1001 Facts
for Your Catholic Geography Bee

Kerry and Nancy MacArthur

Participant/Student Book

Catholic Heritage Curricula
P.O. Box 579090
Modesto, CA 95357
www.chcweb.com   1-800-490-7713

About the Authors

Kerry and Nancy MacArthur are homeschooling parents of five. Kerry has a Bachelor of Arts degree in English from St. John's University in Minnesota and a Master's degree and PhD in English from the University of Notre Dame. He is currently Associate Professor of English at the University of St. Thomas in Houston, TX, and served as English Department Chairman from 1997 till 2001. Nancy has a Bachelor of Science degree from Bemidji State University and has taught art and English in public schools in Minnesota and Texas. They are the authors of the *Pilgrims of the Holy Family* Catholic family activity program.

1001 Facts for Your Catholic Geography Bee was originally developed for geography bees sponsored by the Holy Family Homeschool association of West Houston.

Acknowledgment

We would like to thank the children of Holy Family Homeschool
Association of West Houston for testing this program.

Credit

Cover artwork by Dianne Gotay
Bird and Flower Illustrations by Kim Staggenborg
"Pelican" by the Poor Clare Nuns of Los Altos Hills, CA
"Mary, Patroness of America" by Mary and Rob MacArthur
Catholic-named Cities of the U.S. by Therese Lawrence
Layout and Design by Veronica M. Johnson
Proofreading by Rose M. Decaen

This book is dedicated to
Mary Immaculate,
Patroness of the United States of America.

"Mary, Patroness of America" drawn by Mary (13) and Rob (15) MacArthur

Table of Contents

Introduction

What is geography? It includes a little bit of history, economics, geology, ecology, sociology, and topography all combined to help us understand a place and its inhabitants. God provided great variety and abundance in the North American continent and to this continent have come peoples from all parts of the world. Thus the study of the geography of the United States provides a look at one of the most diverse and varied nations in the world. We hope the use of this book will enrich your family's study of American geography and bring you to a greater appreciation of the blessings God has bestowed upon this nation.

Studying for a Geography Bee

Welcome to your Geography Bee! Whether you have purchased this book to be part of a group bee or whether you will use it within your family, the key to a successful geography bee is to remember to have fun. No one should feel pressure to memorize tons of facts. Memorizing facts from even one category is learning something upon which to build. My own children never liked the idea of a traditional spelling bee in which one misspelled word might put them "out" in a moment's time—after weeks or even months of diligent study. Therefore, I decided to use the categories I had developed and styled my Geography Bee along the lines of the Jeopardy game, in which missing a question simply means missing points.

If you are participating in a Geography Bee, your coordinator will advise you as to which particular categories will be used. The Coordinator/Parent Book contains over 1,000 questions covering 9 categories. The questions are divided into 3 levels: Level 1 is intended for first to third grade children, Level 2 for fourth to sixth graders, and Level 3 for seventh graders and above.

At the time of the Geography Bee, the participant will select from the available categories and be given a question to answer. Frequently, multiple choice answers are offered, especially in the questions for Levels 1 and 2. Consider the following illustration:

Participant: "I'll choose State Capital."

Questioner: "All right; here's your question.

(Level 1)   Minnesota's capital city is named for the apostle whose letters we often hear in the second reading at Mass. Is it St. David, St. Paul, or St. Lucy?"

(Level 2)   Minnesota's capital is named for the apostle who was struck blind by light and fell from his horse. Was it St. Peter, St. Paul, or St. Cecilia?"

(Level 3)   Although Minnesota is nicknamed "Land of 10,000 Lakes," it actually has more than 15,000, including several in its capital city, which is named for a saint. Name Minnesota's capital."

The answer will be fairly obvious to children who have been studying.

Spreadsheets

The Spreadsheets (pages 5-9) list all 13 categories at a glance. It would be overwhelming to try to memorize all categories; therefore, there are no questions provided in the Coordinator/Parent Book for Admission Date, State Name Derivation, State Motto, or State Industry.

The parent may quiz the student using these Spreadsheets, furnishing many clues in a sort of "Name That State" fashion, such as, "Which state has the Purple Finch as state bird, the lilac as state flower, the White Birch as state tree, Concord as its capital, and is nicknamed 'The Granite State'?"

Study Sheets

The Study Sheets (pages 11-57) furnish information on one category at a time. Many of the questions in the Bee are based on the "To Learn More" section in the Study Sheets.

A good place to begin is by memorizing the state capitals, since the capital is sometimes given as a hint in questions in other categories.

State Profile Work Sheets

State Profile Work Sheets (pages 58-59) have been provided as a visual aid and for hands-on learning. The master work sheet (page 59) may be copied for each state the student is studying. The State Profile Work Sheet can be completed as students use the Study Sheets (pages 11-58) to memorize the state facts. Students may color and paste on the state flower and bird (pages 61-71), draw freehand or paste on the state map (pages 73-97), and fill in the state's profile. A sample has been completed on page 58. Depending on the student's ability, details may be added to the map, such as, rivers, capital, landmark, topography, and missionary travels. State flag stickers may be purchased to apply next to the state's name. These would also make a good reward once the child has correctly completed a State Profile Work Sheet.

When completed, the State Profile Work Sheet may be placed in a "U.S. Geography Binder." Give children their own three-ring binder or notebook. Encourage children to add to their binder as they learn new facts. For each state, students may draw a full page map, flag, bird, and flower; write an essay on a famous native or missionary; mark the homes of relatives and pen-pals; add climate, topography, and weather information as it is learned. The ideas are endless, making a Geography Binder a solid reference and foundation for further geography studies!

Students will enjoy occasionally "testing" their knowledge by trying to complete a State Profile Work Sheet from memory. Use the Spreadsheets (pages 5-9) as an answer key to correct state profiles.

Map Work Sheets

The maps furnished in the last part of the book (pages 73-97) may be used in a number of ways.

1) To teach recognition of the states by their shapes.

2) To write within each shape that state's name and/or capital, bird, flower, tree, Catholic fact, etc.

3) To test knowledge.

4) To complete the State Profile Work Sheets (pages 58-59).

Copy the U.S. map master (page 99) for quick State Shape drills and charting expeditions (Lewis and Clark); routes (Cumberland Trail, Pony Express); missionary travels (Fr. Marquette, Fr. De Smet); and more.

Ways to Study

In addition to rote memorization, my children also benefited from inexpensive methods to enliven their study. For example, to study each state's capital, I cut out 100 small rectangles of posterboard, wrote state names on 50 of them and the capital names on the remaining 50. The 100 rectangles were mixed and drawn out one at a time from a box and placed face up in front of the child. When a card (either a state name or a capital) was drawn, the child had to pair it correctly with its matching card. For example, the capital card "Sacramento" had to be matched with the "California" state card. Re-use the 50 state name cards and just make up 50 more with your next category's matches.

On another occasion we posted a large U.S. map, and the children tried to place in each state small pictures of the state bird, flower, and tree that I had copied from other sources. Little bits of masking tape or Sticky Tac on the back of each picture should not mar the map. Pictures of the State Flower and Bird can be found on pages 61-71.

And, of course, a family should always feel free to use any games, puzzles, videos, computer aids or programs, etc., to make learning fun! There are website resources listed on page 105.

Your coordinator will keep you informed concerning the details of your particular Geography Bee. Throughout your study, dedicate your time to Our Mother, Mary Immaculate, Patroness of the United States. She will be pleased with your efforts to learn more about the great resources of our land and its Catholic heritage.

Nancy MacArthur
Houston, Texas

O God, through the hands of Mary Immaculate we wish to thank You for the great resources of this land and for the freedom which has been its heritage. Through the intercession of Mary, have mercy on the Catholic Church in America. Mary, Immaculate Virgin, Our Mother, Patroness of our land, we praise you, honor you, and give ourselves to you. Protect us from every harm. Pray for us, that acting always according to your will and the Will of your Divine Son, we may live and die pleasing to God. Amen.

STATE	NAME DERIVATION	FAMOUS NATIVE	MOTTO	LANDMARK
Alabama	Alibamu Indian, "plant gatherer"	Helen Keller	We Dare Defend Our Rights	Tuskegee Institute
Alaska	Aleutian Indian, "mainland"	Edgar Nollner	North to the Future	Mount McKinley
Arizona	Papago Indian, "small spring"	Geronimo	God Enriches	Grand Canyon
Arkansas	Quapaw, "downstream people"	Douglas MacArthur	The People Rule	Crater of Diamonds
California	Treasure island in a Spanish story	Richard Nixon	Eureka!	Death Valley
Colorado	Spanish, "red"	Jack Dempsey	Nothing Without Providence	Pikes Peak
Connecticut	Algonquin, "beside long, tidal river"	Harriet Beecher Stowe	He Who Transplanted Still Sustains	Mystic Seaport
Delaware	Lord De La Warr	Pierre Du Pont	Liberty and Independence	Chesapeake & Delaware Canal
Florida	Spanish, "Easter" (Pascua florida)	Sidney Poitier	In God We Trust	Everglades National Park
Georgia	King George II of England	Martin Luther King, Jr.	Wisdom, Justice, and Moderation	Stone Mountain
Hawaii	King HawaiiLoa	King Kamehameha	The Life of the Land is Perpetuated in Righteousness	Mauna Loa
Idaho	Shoshone Indian, "Sun is coming up"	Ezra Pound	It is Perpetual	Hell's Canyon
Illinois	Algonquian Indian, "man, warrior"	Archbishop Fulton J. Sheen	State Sovereignty, National Union	Sears Tower
Indiana	"Land of Indians"	Wilbur Wright	The Crossroads of America	Indianapolis Motor Speedway
Iowa	Iowa Indian, "one who puts to sleep"	Herbert Hoover	Our Liberties We Prize, Our Rights We Will Maintain	Grotto of the Redemption
Kansas	Dakota Indian, "south wind"	Amelia Earhart	To the Stars Through Difficulties	Dodge City
Kentucky	Cherokee, "dark, bloody ground"	Abraham Lincoln	United We Stand, Divided We Fall	Fort Knox
Louisiana	King Louis XIV of France	Louis Armstrong	Union, Justice, and Confidence	The French Quarter
Maine	"Mainland"	Henry W. Longfellow	I Direct	Portland Head Light
Maryland	BVM; Queen Henrietta Maria	Francis Scott Key	Manly Deeds, Womanly Words	U.S. Naval Academy
Massachusetts	Mass. Indian, "place of great hill"	Clara Barton	By Sword We Seek Peace, But Peace Only Under Liberty	Plymouth Rock
Michigan	Ojibway Indian, "great lake"	Henry Ford	If You Seek a Pleasant Peninsula, Look About You	Automobile Factories
Minnesota	Dakota Indian, "sky-colored waters"	Judy Garland	The Star of the North	Source of Mississippi River
Mississippi	Indian, "father of waters"	William Faulkner	By Valor and Arms	Vicksburg
Missouri	Indian, "town of large canoes"	Jesse James	The Welfare of the People Shall be the Supreme Law	Mark Twain's Home
Montana	Spanish, "mountainous"	Gary Cooper	Gold and Silver	Little Bighorn Battlefield
Nebraska	Oto Indian, "flat water"	Gerald Ford	Equality Before the Law	Chimney Rock
Nevada	Spanish, "snow clad"	Wovoka (Jack Wilson)	All for Our Country	Hoover Dam
New Hampshire	Hampshire County in England	Alan Shepard, Jr.	Live Free or Die	Mount Washington
New Jersey	Isle of Jersey in Engl. Channel	James Fenimore Cooper	Liberty and Prosperity	Atlantic City Boardwalk
New Mexico	Honoring Mexico	Maria Martinez	It Grows as it Goes	Carlsbad Caverns
New York	Duke of York (future James II)	Theodore Roosevelt	Excelsior	Statue of Liberty
North Carolina	King Charles I of England	Virginia Dare	To Be Rather Than To Seem	Great Smokey Mountain Natl. Park
North Dakota	Dakota, "allies"	Lawrence Welk	Liberty & Union, Now & Forever, One & Inseparable	Geographic Center of North America
Ohio	Iroquois Indian, "something great"	Thomas Edison	With God, All Things Are Possible	Pro Football Hall of Fame
Oklahoma	Choctaw Indian, "people, red"	Will Rogers	Labor Conquers All Things	Horse Show Capital of World
Oregon	French, "hurricane"	Chief Joseph	The Union	Crater Lake
Pennsylvania	Wm. Penn; Latin, "woods"	Daniel Boone	Virtue, Liberty, and Independence	Liberty Bell
Rhode Island	Isle of Rhodes in Aegean Sea	Gilbert Charles Stuart	Hope	Narragansett Bay
South Carolina	King Charles I of England	Andrew Jackson	While I Breathe, I Hope	Fort Sumter
South Dakota	Dakota, "allies"	Hubert Humphrey	Under God the People Rule	Mount Rushmore
Tennessee	Cherokee village "Tanasie"	Davy Crockett	Agriculture and Commerce	Grand Ole Opry
Texas	Tejas Indian, "friendship"	Dwight Eisenhower	Friendship	The Alamo
Utah	Ute Indians	Loretta Young	Industry	Great Salt Lake
Vermont	French, "green mountains"	Calvin Coolidge	Freedom and Unity	Green Mountain National Forest
Virginia	Queen Elizabeth I of England	Lewis & Clark	Thus Always to Tyrants	Williamsburg
Washington	George Washington	Bing Crosby	By and By	Mount St. Helens
West Virginia	Queen Elizabeth I of England	Chuck Yeager	Mountaineers are Always Free	Harpers Ferry
Wisconsin	Indian, "gathering of waters"	Frank Lloyd Wright	Forward	Wisconsin Dells
Wyoming	Delaware Indian, "on the great plain"	Jackson Pollack	Equal Rights	Yellowstone National Park

STATE	CATHOLIC FACT	HISTORICAL FACT	INDUSTRY
Alabama	Ave Maria Grotto replicas	Montgomery site of first Confederate capital	Steel, cotton lint, coal
Alaska	Christ the King Statue on King Island	Bought for $7.2 million in 1867	Processed fish, dairy, petroleum, mining
Arizona	Mission San Xavier del Bac	Oldest continuously inhabited site—Oraibi—1100s	Electric equipment, cattle, copper, cotton
Arkansas	Shrine of Our Lady of the Ozarks	De Soto explored in 1541	Processed foods, cotton, petroleum
California	Bl. Junipero Serra's missions	Discovery of gold at Sutter's Mill	Machinery, vegetables & fruit, petroleum, electronics
Colorado	Sacred Heart Shrine near Golden	Gold discovered at Cherry Creek in 1858	Machinery, cattle, petroleum, wheat
Connecticut	Priests not permitted until 1818	First nuclear submarine built and launched at Groton	Machinery, dairy, soybeans, stone
Delaware	First mission before 1750	First state to ratify U.S. Constitution	Chemicals, broiler chickens, sand and gravel
Florida	St. Augustine, first Catholic parish in U.S.	St. Augustine, oldest continuously settled town	Processed foods, oranges, phosphate, tourism
Georgia	Flannery O'Connor born in Savannah	Capture of Atlanta, turning point of Civil War	Textile mill products, broiler chickens, clays
Hawaii	Bl. Damien de Veuster's ministry to lepers	Japanese attacked Pearl Harbor	Processed foods, sugarcane, sand & gravel, tourism
Idaho	Sacred Heart Mission, oldest building in Idaho	First electricity generated from nuclear energy	Processed foods, potatoes, cattle, silver
Illinois	St. Francis Cabrini died in Chicago	Chicago fire of 1871	Steel, corn, coal
Indiana	Fr. Julius Nieuwland developed neoprene	Battle of Tippecanoe led by William H. Harrison	Electrical equipment, corn, coal, hogs
Iowa	Luxembourgian settlers founded St. Donatus	First U.S. center for study of child development	Nonelectric machinery, hogs, stone, corn
Kansas	St. Philippine Duchesne worked with Potawatomi	Quantrill's raid on Lawrence in Civil War	Transportation equipment, wheat, petroleum, cattle
Kentucky	Bardstown, first Catholic settlement	Daniel Boone arrived in 1769	Whiskey, tobacco, coal, cattle
Louisiana	St. John Berchmans's miracle to Mary Wilson	Battle of New Orleans led by Andrew Jackson	Chemicals, rice, petroleum
Maine	Site of first Mass offered in New England	Doughnut hole invented in 1847	Paper products, potatoes, cement, seafood
Maryland	First English colony to permit the Mass	Francis Scott Key wrote the "Star-Spangled Banner"	Food products, poultry, seafood, coal
Massachusetts	Annual blessing of fishing fleet	Revolutionary War began	Electrical equipment, dairy, sand & gravel, seafood
Michigan	St. Isaac Jogues preached near Sault Ste. Marie	Henry Ford's first automobile factory	Motor vehicles, dairy, iron ore, fruit
Minnesota	Fr Hennepin named St. Anthony Falls (Mpls.)	Schoolcraft discovered source of Mississippi	Chemicals, corn, iron ore
Mississippi	Site of first seminary to admit African-Americans	Vicksburg captured after 47-day siege in 1863	Clothing, cotton, petroleum
Missouri	St. Philippine Duchesne died in St. Charles	Start of Oregon and Santa Fe trails	Transportation equipment, soybeans, lead
Montana	Fr. De Smet established first mission	Custer's Last Stand at Little Bighorn in 1876	Copper products, cattle, copper, wheat
Nebraska	Priestly Fraternity of St. Peter est. seminary--1998	First Arbor Day celebrated in 1872	Food products, cattle, petroleum
Nevada	Former gold miner, Fr. Monogue, missionary	Kit Carson guided Frémont expedition—1843-45	Food products, cattle, barite, tourism
New Hampshire	NH constitution barred Catholic officeholders	Oldest tax-supported free library	Nonelectrical equipment, dairy, sand and gravel
New Jersey	Headquarters of the Blue Army of Fatima	Victory at Trenton for George Washington	Chemicals, vegetables and fruit, stone
New Mexico	Shrine of Our Lord of Esquipulas	Oldest Road—Santa Fe to Chihuahua	Petroleum, cattle, natural gas
New York	National Shrine of North American Martyrs	Nation's first capital at New York City	Printing and publishing, dairy, stone
North Carolina	First Catholic church not built until 1823	First airplane flight at Kitty Hawk	Textiles, tobacco, stone
North Dakota	Fr. Dumoulin was first Catholic missionary	Explorer de la Verendrye arrived in 1738	Machinery, wheat, petroleum
Ohio	Shrine of the Holy Relics, largest collection in world	Commodore Perry secured Lake Erie in 1812	Transportation equipment, corn, coal
Oklahoma	Abbey of Fontgombault est. daughter house—1999	Biggest land run—50,000 settlers on 9/16/1893	Nonelectric machinery, cattle, petroleum
Oregon	Fr. Blanchet celebrated first Mass in 1838	Lewis and Clark's westernmost explorations	Wood products, cattle, sand and gravel
Pennsylvania	Former Russian Prince, Fr. Gallitzin, est. Loretto	Declaration of Independence signed	Metal foundry industries, dairy, coal
Rhode Island	First Catholic Church not built until 1829	First gas lamps introduced in Newport	Metal foundries, dairy
South Carolina	Missionary attempt as early as 1569	Civil War began at Fort Sumter	Textile mill products, tobacco, cement
South Dakota	Fr. Ravoux published Dakota language prayer book	"Wild Bill" Hickok shot in Deadwood	Food products, cattle, gold
Tennessee	Replica of Shrine at Banneux, Belgium	Battle of Shiloh claimed 23,000 casualties	Chemicals, tobacco, stone
Texas	Explorer La Salle's priests martyred	1900 hurricane killed 6,000 people	Chemicals, cattle, petroleum
Utah	First known missionary priests arrived in 1776	Meeting site of Transcontinental Railroad	Food products, barley, asphalt, mining
Vermont	Ethan Allen's daughter converted and became nun	Northernmost land action of Civil War—St. Albans	Machines and tools, dairy, granite
Virginia	Missionary attempt as early as 1526	Appomattox surrender ended Civil War	Chemicals, cattle, coal, dairy
Washington	First missionary priests arrived in 1838	Grand Coulee Dam completed in 1942	Aircraft and aerospace systems, wheat, coal, timber
West Virginia	First Catholic church founded in 1835	John Brown's raid on Harpers Ferry in 1859	Chemicals, dairy, coal
Wisconsin	Fr. Marquette erected cross at site of Holy Hill	First typewriter designed in Milwaukee in 1867	Engines, dairy, sand and gravel
Wyoming	Fr. De Smet celebrated first Mass in 1840	Yellowstone became first U.S. National Park	Petroleum products, cattle, petroleum

STATE	ADMISSION DATE	CAPITAL	FLOWER	BIRD	NICKNAME	TREE
Alabama	Dec. 14, 1819	Montgomery	Camellia	Yellowhammer	Yellowhammer State	Southern Pine
Alaska	Jan. 3, 1959	Juneau	Forget-me-not	Willow Ptarmigan	The Great Land	Sitka Spruce
Arizona	Feb. 14, 1912	Phoenix	Saguaro Cactus Blossom	Cactus Wren	Grand Canyon State	Paloverde
Arkansas	June 15, 1836	Little Rock	Apple Blossom	Mockingbird	Land of Opportunity	Southern Pine
California	Sept. 9, 1850	Sacramento	California Poppy	California Quail	Golden State	California Redwood
Colorado	Aug. 1, 1876	Denver	Rocky Mtn. Columbine	Lark Bunting	Centennial State	Blue Spruce
Connecticut	Jan. 9, 1788	Hartford	Mountain Laurel	Robin	Constitution State	White Oak
Delaware	Dec. 7, 1787	Dover	Peach Blossom	Blue Hen Chicken	First State	American Holly
Florida	Mar. 3, 1845	Tallahassee	Orange Blossom	Mockingbird	Sunshine State	Sabal Palm
Georgia	Jan. 2, 1788	Atlanta	Cherokee Rose	Brown Thrasher	Peach State	Live Oak
Hawaii	Aug. 21, 1959	Honolulu	Hibiscus	Hawaiian Goose	Aloha State	Kukui
Idaho	July 3, 1890	Boise	Syringa	Mountain Bluebird	Gem State	Western White Pine
Illinois	Dec. 3, 1818	Springfield	Violet	Cardinal	Land of Lincoln	White Oak
Indiana	Dec. 11, 1816	Indianapolis	Peony	Cardinal	Hoosier State	Tulip Tree
Iowa	Dec. 28, 1846	Des Moines	Wild Rose	Eastern Goldfinch	Hawkeye State	Oak
Kansas	Jan. 29, 1861	Topeka	Sunflower	Western Meadowlark	Sunflower State	Cottonwood
Kentucky	June 1, 1792	Frankfort	Goldenrod	Cardinal	Bluegrass State	Kentucky Coffee Tree
Louisiana	Apr. 30, 1812	Baton Rouge	Magnolia	Brown Pelican	Pelican State	Bald Cypress
Maine	Mar. 15, 1820	Augusta	White Pine Cone & Tassel	Black-capped Chickadee	Pine Tree State	Eastern White Pine
Maryland	Apr. 28, 1788	Annapolis	Black-eyed Susan	Baltimore Oriole	Old Line State	White Oak
Massachusetts	Feb. 6, 1788	Boston	Mayflower	Black-capped Chickadee	Bay State	American Elm
Michigan	Jan. 26, 1837	Lansing	Apple Blossom	Robin	Great Lakes State	Eastern White Pine
Minnesota	May 11, 1858	St. Paul	Showy Lady's Slipper	Common Loon	Land of 10,000 Lakes	Norway Pine
Mississippi	Dec. 10, 1817	Jackson	Magnolia	Mockingbird	Magnolia State	Magnolia
Missouri	Aug. 10, 1821	Jefferson City	Red Hawthorn	Eastern Bluebird	Show Me State	Flowering Dogwood
Montana	Nov. 8, 1889	Helena	Bitterroot	Western Meadowlark	Treasure State	Ponderosa Pine
Nebraska	Mar. 1, 1867	Lincoln	Goldenrod	Western Meadowlark	Cornhusker State	Cottonwood
Nevada	Oct. 31, 1864	Carson City	Sagebrush	Mountain Bluebird	Silver State	Single-leaf Piñon
New Hampshire	June 21, 1788	Concord	Lilac	Purple Finch	Granite State	White Birch
New Jersey	Dec. 18, 1787	Trenton	Violet	American Goldfinch	Garden State	Red Oak
New Mexico	Jan. 6, 1912	Santa Fe	Yucca Blossom	Roadrunner	Land of Enchantment	Piñon Pine
New York	July 26, 1788	Albany	Rose	Eastern Bluebird	Empire State	Sugar Maple
North Carolina	Nov. 21, 1789	Raleigh	Flowering Dogwood	Cardinal	Tarheel State	Southern Pine
North Dakota	Nov. 2, 1889	Bismarck	Wild Prairie Rose	Western Meadowlark	Peace Garden State	American Elm
Ohio	Mar. 1, 1803	Columbus	Red Carnation	Cardinal	Buckeye State	Buckeye
Oklahoma	Nov. 16, 1907	Oklahoma City	Mistletoe	Scissor-tailed Flycatcher	Sooner State	Redbud
Oregon	Feb. 14, 1859	Salem	Oregon Grape	Western Meadowlark	Beaver State	Douglas Fir
Pennsylvania	Dec. 12, 1787	Harrisburg	Mountain Laurel	Ruffed Grouse	Keystone State	Hemlock
Rhode Island	May 29, 1790	Providence	Violet	Rhode Island Red	Ocean State	Red Maple
South Carolina	May 23, 1788	Columbia	Carolina Jessamine	Carolina Wren	Palmetto State	Palmetto
South Dakota	Nov. 2, 1889	Pierre	Pasqueflower	Ring-necked Pheasant	Coyote State	Black Hills Spruce
Tennessee	June 1, 1796	Nashville	Iris	Mockingbird	Volunteer State	Tulip Poplar
Texas	Dec. 29, 1845	Austin	Bluebonnet	Mockingbird	Lone Star State	Pecan
Utah	Jan. 4, 1896	Salt Lake City	Sego Lily	California Gull	Beehive State	Blue Spruce
Vermont	Mar. 4, 1791	Montpelier	Red Clover	Hermit Thrush	Green Mountain State	Sugar Maple
Virginia	June 25, 1788	Richmond	Flowering Dogwood	Cardinal	Old Dominion State	Flowering Dogwood
Washington	Nov. 11, 1889	Olympia	Rhododendron	American Goldfinch	Evergreen State	Western Hemlock
West Virginia	June 20, 1863	Charleston	Rhododendron Maximum	Cardinal	Mountain State	Sugar Maple
Wisconsin	May 29, 1848	Madison	Wood Violet	Robin	Badger State	Sugar Maple
Wyoming	July 10, 1890	Cheyenne	Indian Paintbrush	Western Meadowlark	Equality State	Cottonwood

State Capital

Alabama — Montgomery
Alaska — Juneau
Arizona — Phoenix
Arkansas — Little Rock
California — Sacramento
Colorado — Denver
Connecticut — Hartford
Delaware — Dover
Florida — Tallahassee
Georgia — Atlanta
Hawaii — Honolulu
Idaho — Boise
Illinois — Springfield
Indiana — Indianapolis
Iowa — Des Moines
Kansas — Topeka
Kentucky — Frankfort
Louisiana — Baton Rouge
Maine — Augusta
Maryland — Annapolis
Massachusetts — Boston
Michigan — Lansing
Minnesota — St. Paul
Mississippi — Jackson
Missouri — Jefferson City

Montana — Helena
Nebraska — Lincoln
Nevada — Carson City
New Hampshire — Concord
New Jersey — Trenton
New Mexico — Santa Fe
New York — Albany
North Carolina — Raleigh
North Dakota — Bismarck
Ohio — Columbus
Oklahoma — Oklahoma City
Oregon — Salem
Pennsylvania — Harrisburg
Rhode Island — Providence
South Carolina — Columbia
South Dakota — Pierre
Tennessee — Nashville
Texas — Austin
Utah — Salt Lake City
Vermont — Montpelier
Virginia — Richmond
Washington — Olympia
West Virginia — Charleston
Wisconsin — Madison
Wyoming — Cheyenne

Do You Know?
Which state's capital is named after the Blessed Sacrament?

State Flower

Alabama — Camellia	Montana — Bitterroot
Alaska — Forget-me-not	Nebraska — Goldenrod
Arizona — Saguaro Cactus Blossom	Nevada — Sagebrush
Arkansas — Apple Blossom	New Hampshire — Lilac
California — California Poppy	New Jersey — Violet
Colorado — Rocky Mountain Columbine	New Mexico — Yucca Blossom
Connecticut — Mountain Laurel	New York — Rose
Delaware — Peach Blossom	North Carolina — Flowering Dogwood
Florida — Orange Blossom	North Dakota — Wild Prairie Rose
Georgia — Cherokee Rose	Ohio — Red Carnation
Hawaii — Hibiscus	Oklahoma — Mistletoe
Idaho — Syringa	Oregon — Oregon Grape
Illinois — Violet	Pennsylvania — Mountain Laurel
Indiana — Peony	Rhode Island — Violet
Iowa — Wild Rose	South Carolina — Carolina Jessamine
Kansas — Sunflower	South Dakota — Pasqueflower
Kentucky — Goldenrod	Tennessee — Iris
Louisiana — Magnolia	Texas — Bluebonnet
Maine — White Pine Cone and Tassel	Utah — Sego Lily
Maryland — Black-eyed Susan	Vermont — Red Clover
Massachusetts — Mayflower	Virginia — Flowering Dogwood
Michigan — Apple Blossom	Washington — Rhododendron
Minnesota — Showy Lady's Slipper	West Virginia — Rhododendron Maximum
Mississippi — Magnolia	Wisconsin — Wood Violet
Missouri — Red Hawthorn	Wyoming — Indian Paintbrush

To Learn More . . .

Alabama — Camellia — Tea Family
The Camellia is a flowering shrub imported from China and Japan. They are evergreen, with large, showy white or red flowers, blooming in winter and spring. They are cultivated as ornamentals throughout the South and the southern Pacific coast.

Alaska — Forget-me-not — Borage Family
These wildflowers have teardrop-shaped leaves and small, 5-petaled, light-blue flowers. They prefer stream banks and wet soil. Traditionally the forget-me-not symbolized fidelity in love.

Arizona — Saguaro Cactus Blossom — Cactus Family
The Saguaro, or giant, cactus can grow to over thirty feet tall in the desert Southwest. It has a large, showy white blossom. The range of the saguaro has been much reduced due to theft and attempts at transplanting.

Arkansas — Apple Blossom — Rose Family
The apple is a very widespread tree found in both cultivated and wild forms. It is one of the most common and popular fruits in the world. Apple trees may grow up to thirty feet tall. They bloom in the spring and produce a heavy cover of white or pink blossoms of 5 petals.

The apple is traditionally associated with the forbidden fruit of the Garden of Eden, perhaps because the Latin word for apple ("malum") is almost identical to the Latin word for evil. When an artist includes an apple in a depiction of the Madonna and Child, it is intended to remind us of their roles as the New Eve and New Adam.

California — California Poppy — Poppy Family
The California Poppy is a wild poppy with yellow blossoms which grows in California and Oregon.

Colorado — Rocky Mountain Columbine — Buttercup Family

Columbines are striking flowers with 5 spurred, cone-shaped petals. The Rocky Mountain variety's blossoms are larger than those of most columbines and are a bright blue color. Main types of columbine have purplish flowers and therefore symbolize sorrow. However, the blossom's dove-like appearance ("columbine" means "dove-like") is associated with the Holy Spirit. Artists may introduce the columbine to refer to the Holy Spirit or to the Seven Gifts of the Holy Spirit.

Connecticut — Mountain Laurel — Heath Family

The Mountain Laurel is a shrub or small tree with pointed, oval leaves. The blossoms are star-shaped and about 1 inch across. They are white or pink, with purple markings inside.

Delaware — Peach Blossom — Rose Family

Peach trees are important fruit trees that have grown both in the wild and cultivated forms in the American Southeast. The peach blossom is white to deep pink and appears in the spring before the leaves. The peach can be used to symbolize charity.

Florida — Orange Blossom — Rue Family

The orange is one of the most important fruit trees in the world, and Florida is one of the two leading orange-producing states in the U.S. The blossoms are white and very fragrant. In tradition orange blossoms were formerly associated with weddings.

Georgia — Cherokee Rose — Rose Family

The Cherokee rose is a white-blossomed wild rose. Wild roses usually have a single set of 5 petals.

Hawaii — Hibiscus — Mallow Family

The hibiscus is a flowering shrub of the tropical climate. The blossoms are large (3 to 4 inches across), trumpet-shaped, and are usually pink or red, though horticulturists have produced other colors.

Idaho — Syringa — Saxifrage Family

The syringa is a flowering shrub that grows throughout Idaho. It bears clusters of white, 4-petaled blossoms.

Illinois — Violet — Violet Family

The violet is a small, low-growing flower, mostly of woodlands. It has heart-shaped leaves and 4 or 5 petals of a purple, white, or yellow color. In Christian art the violet symbolizes humility.

Indiana — Peony — Ranunculus Family

The peony is a popular garden flower and is found across the Midwest. Most grow 2 to 3 inches in height; have large, glossy leaves; and have large, round blossoms 5 to 6 inches in diameter, usually white or light pink in color.

Iowa — Wild Rose — Rose Family

The wild rose is a low-growing flower of the prairies. The bristly stem holds pink blossoms of 5 petals. These 5 petals symbolize the 5 Joys of Mary and the letters in her name: Maria.

Kansas — Sunflower — Daisy Family

The sunflower, a North American native, has been cultivated since long before Europeans came to the Western Hemisphere. The plants are very tall, up to 15 feet, and the flower disc is very large, sometimes a foot across. The disc has a dark center which is ringed by bright yellow leaves.

Kentucky — Goldenrod — Daisy Family

The goldenrod is a common wild flower of eastern and mid-western fields and roadsides, blooming in late summer to fall. The plant is usually 1 to 3 inches tall with long, willow-shaped leaves, and clusters of gold-yellow blossoms at the top.

Louisiana — Magnolia — Magnolia Family

Magnolias are evergreen trees of a very ancient kind, growing from 30 to 80 feet tall. They have large glossy leaves. The blossoms are large, too, 6 to 9 inches in diameter and very fragrant, with white, creamy-textured petals. After blossoming, the magnolia develops a large seed pod with individual cavities from which the red seeds hang by threads when ripe.

Maine — White Pine Cone and Tassel — Pine Family

For its state flower Maine has chosen parts of its state tree, the tassel and the cone (seed pod).

Maryland — Black-eyed Susan — Daisy Family

The Black-eyed Susan is a 1- to 3-foot tall daisy-like flower with yellow petals ringing a dark brown center. It grows in meadows and open woods.

Massachusetts — Mayflower — Blueberry Family

The mayflower, better known as the trailing arbutus, is a low-growing flower of boggy or sandy forests. It has oblong, evergreen leaves and light-pink or white, fragrant blossoms.

Michigan — Apple Blossom — Rose Family
See Arkansas.

Minnesota — Showy Lady's Slipper — Orchid Family
The showy lady's slipper is a rare orchid of the north woods and bogs. It has a few large, oblong leaves close to the ground. The characteristic flower, with 3 white petals above and a pink pouch below, blooms on a stalk above the leaves. The name for this group of flowers — Lady's Slipper — is short for "Our Lady's Slipper" because the pouch portion of the blossom was thought to resemble a shoe or slipper.

Mississippi — Magnolia — Magnolia Family
See Louisiana.

Missouri — Red Hawthorn — Rose Family
The hawthorn is a shrub or small tree. It has toothed leaves and thorns on its branches. The blossom is similar to that of the apple with white petals and either red or yellow stamens. The fruit resemble small apples.

Montana — Bitterroot — Purslane Family
The bitterroot is found in the northwest part of the U.S. It has succulent leaves and a single pink radial blossom. The fleshy root, in spite of its bitter flavor, is edible and is considered a delicacy.

Nebraska — Goldenrod — Daisy Family
See Kentucky.

Nevada — Sagebrush — Daisy Family
The sagebrush is a tree or shrub found in western prairies and mountains. The narrow leaves produce a "sage" aroma. The blossoms, arranged in narrow clusters, are small and brownish-yellow.

New Hampshire — Lilac — Olive Family
The lilac is an ornamental shrub or tree native to Eurasia. It has long been popular in landscaping in the northern tier of states. The blossoms are produced in large cone-shaped clusters and are usually light purple and white and very fragrant.

New Jersey — Violet — Violet Family
See Illinois.

New Mexico — Yucca Blossom — Lily Family
The yucca is a plant that grows in near-desert conditions. The spear-like leaves spring directly from the root. A tall stalk (up to 10 feet) rises above and produces a mass of white, bell-shaped flowers.

New York — Rose — Rose Family
The rose has been cultivated for thousands of years in Eurasia and since colonial days in the New World. A wide variety of forms and colors have been developed. The rose usually depicted as New York's state flower is the red rose. In Christian symbolism the rose is the Blessed Virgin Mary's flower, since she herself is the "Rosa Mystica." The white rose stands for the Joyful Mysteries of the rosary, the red rose for the Sorrowful, and the yellow rose for the Glorious. The white rose can also stand for chastity, the red for martyrdom, and the yellow for perfection.

North Carolina — Flowering Dogwood — Dogwood Family
The flowering dogwood is a shrub or small tree with oval leaves. It blooms in the spring. The blossoms are actually quite small and clumped together, but they are surrounded by 4 large, notched, white, petal-like bracts.

North Dakota — Wild Prairie Rose — Rose Family
The prairie rose is a variety of wild rose with pink petals. *See Iowa.*

Ohio — Red Carnation — Pink Family
The carnation has been a popular garden flower since before 300 B.C., when it was cultivated by the Greeks. Many varieties and colors have been produced. Ohio has chosen the red carnation as its symbol. In art the carnation can represent pure love and can be seen in pictures of betrothals or weddings. It is also associated with the Passion of Christ and with Mary's tears.

Oklahoma — Mistletoe — Mistletoe Family
The mistletoe is a parasitic plant that grows on various deciduous trees. It is evergreen, has small, inconspicuous white flowers, and produces small, white berries. It is traditionally associated with the Christmas season.

Oregon — Oregon Grape — Barberry Family
The Oregon grape is an evergreen shrub that grows to 6 inches in height. It has dark green leaves and yellow flowers, which produce edible blue-black berries.

Pennsylvania — Mountain Laurel — Heath Family
See Connecticut.

Rhode Island — Violet — Violet Family
See Illinois.

South Carolina — Carolina Jessamine — Logania Family

The Carolina jessamine (or jasmine) is not a true jasmine, which would be a member of the olive family. It is a vine with bright yellow, 5-petaled blossoms. It is a popular ornamental of southern gardens, arbors, and fences.

South Dakota — Pasqueflower — Buttercup Family

The pasqueflower is a low-growing flower that blooms in the spring. Its blossom has 6 pointed, light-pink petals surrounding a bright orange-yellow stamen and pistil. The leaves appear after the plant has bloomed. It derives its name from the Easter or Paschal (Pasque) season because it blooms at that time.

Tennessee — Iris — Iris Family

The iris is a plant of moist meadows or low stream banks. The sword-like leaves rise directly from the ground. The blossoms are large and showy, with 3 large, oval, drooping petals (falls) and 3 smaller, more pointed and more upright petals (standards) above. The petals are usually a light-purple color and the falls have conspicuous yellow marks at their centers. The iris has become widely cultivated as a garden flower.

In Christian symbolism the iris is associated with the Blessed Virgin Mary in the prophecy of the Crucifixion, probably because it was known to the Romans as the sword lily. It would thus represent Simeon's prophetic words that a sword would pierce Our Lady's Heart.

Texas — Bluebonnet — Legume Family

The bluebonnet is a wild lupine of the southern prairies. It blooms in the spring and some fields are completely carpeted with blue. The blossoms are deep blue, shaped like bonnets, and grow up along the stem.

Utah — Sego Lily — Lily Family

The sego lily is a lily of the western U.S. It is classified with the mariposa ("butterfly") lilies. The blossom has 3 petals shaped like butterfly's wings; they are white with yellow or purple tint.

Vermont — Red Clover — Legume Family

The red clover is a very common plant of meadows and fallow fields. It has oval leaves that grow in groups of 3 (trefoils) and small, round flower heads of pink or red. Because of its 3 leaves, the clover can symbolize the Holy Trinity.

Virginia — Flowering Dogwood — Dogwood Family

See North Carolina.

Washington — Rhododendron — Heath Family

The rhododendron is a shrub or small tree with dark green, glossy leaves. It produces masses of showy white to pink blossoms in the spring.

West Virginia — Rhododendron Maximum — Heath Family

The rhododendron maximum, or great rhododendron, is a common wild bush in the Allegheny Mountains. It has glossy, dark-green evergreen leaves and produces clusters of white to rose blossoms.

Wisconsin — Wood Violet — Violet Family

See Illinois.

Wyoming — Indian Paintbrush — Snapdragon Family

The Indian paintbrush is a wildflower of meadows and prairies. It has narrow leaves radiating from its stalk which is topped with a flare of yellow to red petals. It blooms all summer.

Would you like to plant a Mary Garden?

St. Bernard spoke of Our Lady as "the violet of humility, the lily of chastity, and the rose of charity."

See page 105.

State Bird

Alabama — Yellowhammer
Alaska — Willow Ptarmigan
Arizona — Cactus Wren
Arkansas — Mockingbird
California — California Quail
Colorado — Lark Bunting
Connecticut — Robin
Delaware — Blue Hen Chicken
Florida — Mockingbird
Georgia — Brown Thrasher
Hawaii — Hawaiian Goose
Idaho — Mountain Bluebird
Illinois — Cardinal
Indiana — Cardinal
Iowa — Eastern Goldfinch
Kansas — Western Meadowlark
Kentucky — Cardinal
Louisiana — Brown Pelican
Maine — Black-capped Chickadee
Maryland — Baltimore Oriole
Massachusetts — Black-capped Chickadee
Michigan — Robin
Minnesota — Common Loon
Mississippi — Mockingbird
Missouri — Eastern Bluebird

Montana — Western Meadowlark
Nebraska — Western Meadowlark
Nevada — Mountain Bluebird
New Hampshire — Purple Finch
New Jersey — American Goldfinch
New Mexico — Roadrunner
New York — Eastern Bluebird
North Carolina — Cardinal
North Dakota — Western Meadowlark
Ohio — Cardinal
Oklahoma — Scissor-tailed Flycatcher
Oregon — Western Meadowlark
Pennsylvania — Ruffed Grouse
Rhode Island — Rhode Island Red
South Carolina — Carolina Wren
South Dakota — Ring-necked Pheasant
Tennessee — Mockingbird
Texas — Mockingbird
Utah — California Gull
Vermont — Hermit Thrush
Virginia — Cardinal
Washington — American Goldfinch
West Virginia — Cardinal
Wisconsin — Robin
Wyoming — Western Meadowlark

To Learn More . . .

Alabama — Yellowhammer
The yellowhammer is also known as the yellow-shafted flicker. Flickers are members of the woodpecker family. They are among the only woodpeckers which are seen frequently on the ground, since they enjoy eating ants.

Alaska — Willow Ptarmigan
Ptarmigans are grouse that inhabit arctic or mountainous regions. Their feathers grow in white in the winter for camouflage, but they are brown in the summer. The willow ptarmigan's summer coat is more reddish than that of other ptarmigans.

Arizona — Cactus Wren
The cactus wren is the largest of American wrens. It is only found in the far southwestern part of the U.S. It sometimes nests in holes in saguaro cacti, Arizona's state flower!

Arkansas — Mockingbird
The mockingbird is a very common bird in the southern states. It is capable of imitating the songs of other birds and even of musical phrases whistled or played by people.

California — California Quail
Quail are fairly small, chicken-like birds that usually prefer to stay on the ground rather than fly. The California quail inhabits wooded areas on the West Coast and can be recognized by the "question mark"-shaped plume on its head.

Colorado — Lark Bunting
The lark bunting is a sparrow-sized bird. The male is black with white wing patches, but the female looks much like a sparrow.

Connecticut — Robin
The American robin is a thrush with a familiar rusty-red breast. Its relative, the European robin, is

often depicted in paintings with Christ, particularly in paintings of the Madonna and Child. Legend says that the robin, out of pity, plucked one of the thorns out of Jesus' crown as He walked to Calvary and a drop of blood fell on its breast, marking it forever with red.

Delaware — Blue Hen Chicken
The Blue Andalusian is a breed of chicken. During the Revolutionary War, Captain Caldwell, an officer in a Delaware regiment, declared that an unconquerable game-cock had to be a "blue hen's chicken," and this bird became the mascot of his regiment and later the state.

Florida — Mockingbird
See Arkansas.

Georgia — Brown Thrasher
The brown thrasher is a fairly large, brown bird with a brown-and-white-streaked breast, related to the mockingbird.

Hawaii — Hawaiian Goose
The Hawaiian goose, or nene, is a rare, brown-and-buff-colored goose, which feeds mainly on grasses.

Idaho — Mountain Bluebird
As its name suggests, the mountain bluebird is found mainly at high elevations, in the western mountains. It is distinguished from the other bluebirds by its lack of a rusty breast.

Illinois — Cardinal
The cardinal is a well-known bird in the eastern U.S., related to the finches. The male is bright red in color and is named for its matching the color worn by the Cardinals, the highest prelates of the Catholic Church.

Indiana — Cardinal
See Illinois.

Iowa — Eastern Goldfinch
This popular bird is recognized by its bright yellow body and black cap. It eats seeds, particularly those of the thistle and sunflower. The European goldfinch has red markings on its head and because of these (the color red being associated with blood and because the goldfinch frequents thorny bushes), it has become associated with the Passion of Christ. Artists frequently include the European goldfinch in paintings of the Christ child (though sometimes the bird depicted is the European robin).

Kansas — Western Meadowlark
The western meadowlark is a bird of fields and fence lines. It is distinguished by its bright breast with a black *v*-shaped mark across it.

Kentucky — Cardinal
See Illinois.

Louisiana — Brown Pelican
The brown pelican is smaller and less common than the white pelican. Pelicans catch fish with the help of their well-known throat pouch, but only the brown pelican dives after its prey from flight. In Christian symbolism the pelican is associated with Christ, particularly in the Crucifixion and the Eucharist, because it was formerly believed that pelicans fed their young by pecking their breasts until they bled and then allowing their young to feed on their blood.

Maine — Black-capped Chickadee
Black-capped chickadees are small, friendly birds that are frequently seen at bird feeders. They are recognized by their black cap and throat and white cheeks.

Maryland — Baltimore Oriole
The Baltimore oriole is a colorful orange, black, and white bird that prefers tall shade trees and lives in the eastern half of the U.S. It is named after Lord Baltimore, the patron of the colony of Maryland, because its colors match those in his coat of arms. Maryland was established as a colony to provide a haven for English Catholics.

Massachusetts — Black-capped Chickadee
See Maine.

Michigan — Robin
See Connecticut.

Minnesota — Common Loon
The loon is a large, mostly aquatic bird found in northern latitudes, only where there is plenty of open water. Although it can barely walk, it is a powerful swimmer and dives to great depths to catch fish. The loon has several distinctive calls which can be heard along lakes in the northern summer. Some of these sound like the laughter of a "lunatic," and that is the source of the bird's name.

Mississippi — Mockingbird
See Arkansas.

Missouri — Eastern Bluebird
The eastern bluebird is a small bird that eats mostly insects. The male has a blue back and a rusty-red breast.

Montana — Western Meadowlark
See Kansas.

Nebraska — Western Meadowlark
See Kansas.

Nevada — Mountain Bluebird
As its name suggests, the mountain bluebird is found mainly at high elevations, in the western mountains. It is distinguished from the other bluebirds by its lack of a rusty-colored breast.

New Hampshire — Purple Finch
The purple finch is a bird of the northern woodlands. The male has a wine-colored head, breast, and rump. Purple finches are often seen at bird-feeders in winter.

New Jersey — American Goldfinch
See Iowa.

New Mexico — Roadrunner
The roadrunner is a large, crested bird that lives in the southwest U.S., mostly in arid regions. It is a fast runner and preys on snakes, lizards, and insects. It seldom flies.

New York — Eastern Bluebird
See Missouri.

North Carolina — Cardinal
See Illinois.

North Dakota — Western Meadowlark
See Kansas.

Ohio — Cardinal
See Illinois.

Oklahoma — Scissor-tailed Flycatcher
The scissor-tailed flycatcher is seen mostly in Oklahoma and Texas. The male can be easily distinguished because of its long tail, almost twice as long as its body. In flight the tail is seen to divide into two separate streamers. The scissor-tailed flycatcher is often seen perching on wires along roads looking for insects.

Oregon — Western Meadowlark
See Kansas.

Pennsylvania — Ruffed Grouse
The ruffed grouse is a brown, chicken-like bird of the northern woodlands. The male attracts his mate by making a "drumming" noise with his wings, which carries for great distances.

Rhode Island — Rhode Island Red
The Rhode Island red is a breed of chicken that was developed in the town of Little Compton, Rhode Island.

South Carolina — Carolina Wren
The Carolina wren is the largest eastern wren. It prefers thick underbrush and humid areas.

South Dakota — Ring-necked Pheasant
The ring-necked pheasant was introduced into America for sporting purposes. It has naturalized and now lives across the northern tier of states, but mostly on the central prairies. It is a large bird, with a long tail, and the male has a head of striking green with a white ring around the neck.

Tennessee — Mockingbird
See Arkansas.

Texas — Mockingbird
See Arkansas.

Utah — California Gull
The California gull has gray upper wings with black at the wing ends. It was chosen as Utah's state bird because the first settlers were led to water by the sight of these gulls flying above the lake.

Vermont — Hermit Thrush
The hermit thrush is a small, brown bird of the northern woodlands. It is the only thrush usually seen in the U.S. in the winter.

Virginia — Cardinal
See Illinois.

Washington — American Goldfinch
See Iowa.

West Virginia — Cardinal
See Illinois.

Wisconsin — Robin
See Connecticut.

Wyoming — Western Meadowlark
See Kansas.

The Pelican:
Symbol of the Holy Eucharist

State Nickname

Alabama — Yellowhammer State
Alaska — The Great Land
Arizona — Grand Canyon State
Arkansas — Land of Opportunity
California — Golden State
Colorado — Centennial State
Connecticut — Constitution State
Delaware — First State
Florida — Sunshine State
Georgia — Peach State
Hawaii — Aloha State
Idaho — Gem State
Illinois — Land of Lincoln
Indiana — Hoosier State
Iowa — Hawkeye State
Kansas — Sunflower State
Kentucky — Bluegrass State
Louisiana — Pelican State
Maine — Pine Tree State
Maryland — Old Line State
Massachusetts — Bay State
Michigan — Great Lakes State
Minnesota — Land of 10,000 Lakes
Mississippi — Magnolia State
Missouri — Show Me State

Montana — Treasure State
Nebraska — Cornhusker State
Nevada — Silver State
New Hampshire — Granite State
New Jersey — Garden State
New Mexico — Land of Enchantment
New York — Empire State
North Carolina — Tarheel State
North Dakota — Peace Garden State
Ohio — Buckeye State
Oklahoma — Sooner State
Oregon — Beaver State
Pennsylvania — Keystone State
Rhode Island — Ocean State
South Carolina — Palmetto State
South Dakota — Coyote State
Tennessee — Volunteer State
Texas — Lone Star State
Utah — Beehive State
Vermont — Green Mountain State
Virginia — Old Dominion State
Washington — Evergreen State
West Virginia — Mountain State
Wisconsin — Badger State
Wyoming — Equality State

To Learn More . . .

Alabama — Yellowhammer State
This nickname originated during the Civil War. One day a company of Alabama troops paraded in uniforms trimmed with bits of bright yellow cloth. The soldiers reminded the people of the yellowhammer bird, which has yellow patches under its wings.

Alternative nicknames: The Cotton State, Heart of Dixie

Alaska — The Great Land
This nickname comes from the word "al-ay-ek-sha," used by the people of the Aleutian Islands. It meant "great land" or "main-land." It sounded like A-la-a-ska to early Russian settlers.

Alternative nicknames: The Last Frontier

Arizona — The Grand Canyon State
This nickname recalls one of the Seven Natural Wonders of the World. This giant gorge of the Colorado River is 217 miles long and 1 mile or more deep as it cuts through the rock of northwestern Arizona. The Grand Canyon is famous the world over.

Alternative nicknames: None

Arkansas — The Land of Opportunity
Arkansas claims this nickname because of the opportunities afforded by its many factories, farms, and mines amid rich natural resources.

Alternative nicknames: The Hot Water State, The Razorback State

California — The Golden State
California's gold fields attracted thousands of miners, "the forty-niners," during the gold rush of 1849. Also, this nickname suggests the brilliant sunshine and golden grass of California pastures in the autumn.

Alternative nicknames: None

Colorado — The Centennial State
Colorado joined the Union in 1876, the centennial (100th anniversary) of the Declaration of Independence.

Alternative nicknames: None

Connecticut — The Constitution State
Connecticut delegates to the Constitutional Convention of 1787 worked out the Connecticut Compromise which broke a deadlock over how many men each state should elect to Congress.

Alternative nicknames: The Nutmeg State

Delaware — The First State
On December 7, 1787, Delaware became the first state to approve (ratify) the U.S. Constitution.

Alternative nicknames: The Diamond State

Florida — The Sunshine State
This nickname tells of the large number of sunny days Florida enjoys. On average, the capital, Tallahassee, has 251 sunny days per year and Miami has 238 sunny days.

Alternative nicknames: Peninsula State, The Everglade State

Georgia — The Peach State
Georgia has always been a leading peach producer and is currently third in the nation. There is a Peach County which is in the center of the peach-growing belt that stretches across central Georgia.

Alternative nicknames: The Goober State, The Empire State of the South

Hawaii — The Aloha State
The Hawaiian people's great friendliness to visitors gives Hawaii its nickname. "Aloha" means "love" in the Hawaiian language.

Alternative nicknames: None

Idaho — The Gem State
Although Idaho ranks first in the nation in silver production and is a leader in the production of zinc and lead, it was because of its enormous bounty of natural resources that natives nicknamed it "The Gem State." Other rich mineral deposits, fertile soil, thick forests, abundant plant and animal life, great water supplies, and beautiful mountain ranges, attractive to skiers, make it one "gem of a state."

Alternative nicknames: None

Illinois — Land of Lincoln
The people of Illinois are proud of the fact that Abraham Lincoln lived most of his life in their state, mostly in New Salem and in the capital, Springfield, where he is buried.

Alternative nicknames: The Prairie State

Indiana — The Hoosier State
Although of uncertain meaning, Indiana's nickname may have come from the Indiana settlers' traditional greeting to visitors, "Who's here?" or questioning them about their place of origin, as in "Who's yours [state]?" Some have also suggested that it came from "husher," a slang word for a fighting man who could "hush" others with his fists.

Alternative nicknames: None

Iowa — The Hawkeye State
This nickname honors Black Hawk, the famous Indian chief who led a group of Sauk and Fox Indians against whites in the Black Hawk War of 1832. Indians were defeated and gave up a strip of land known as the Black Hawk Purchase, located along the Mississippi River. Permanent settlement began in 1833.

Alternative nicknames: The Corn State

Kansas — The Sunflower State
In 1999 the state flower of Kansas, the sunflower, yielded a crop of 405,000,000 pounds of sunflower seeds, making the state a leading producer.

Alternative nicknames: The Jayhawk State

Kentucky — The Bluegrass State
An entire 8,000-square-mile area of Kentucky — in the approximate center of Kentucky and extending north to the Ohio River — attracted the earliest settlements and is the state's richest agricultural region. Bluegrass, with its steel-blue tint, forms a dense sod which is very resistant to the trampling from stock and is ranked as the best pasture and lawn grass throughout its range.

Alternative nicknames: None

Louisiana — The Pelican State
This nickname was so given for the many brown pelicans that live in the marshes along the Louisiana coast. An otherwise uncommon bird, smaller and less frequently seen than the white pelican, the brown pelican is the only pelican to dive from mid-flight to pursue its prey.

Alternative nicknames: The Creole State

Maine — The Pine Tree State
Maine gets this nickname from the tall pines that once made up most of the state's forests. Until the late 1700s, the white pine was Maine's greatest resource, mainly used to build ship masts. Today most of Maine's pines are second-growth trees. Forest covers 18 million acres or about 90 percent of the total land area!

Alternative nicknames: None

Maryland — The Old Line State
Maryland's heroic "troops of the line" won praise from General George Washington during the Revolutionary War.

Alternative nicknames: The Free State, The Lumber State, The Pine Tree State

Massachusetts — The Bay State
The Puritans founded their famous colony on Massachusetts Bay, which bounds most of Massachusetts on the east. But numerous other bays contribute to the nickname: Nahant, Boston, Quincy, Hingham, Plymouth, and Cape Cod Bays to the east; Mount Hope and Buzzard's Bays to the south.

Alternative nicknames: The Old Colony State

Michigan — The Great Lakes State
Michigan touches 4 of the 5 Great Lakes — Superior, Huron, Erie, and Michigan. The state's 3,288-mile shoreline is longer than that of any other inland state.

Alternative nicknames: The Wolverine State, Water Wonderland

Minnesota — Land of 10,000 Lakes
Minnesota has one of the greatest water areas of any state. Its thousands of inland lakes cover 4,750 square miles, over a twentieth of the state's area. The number of lakes has been estimated at 22,000, of which more than 15,000 cover 10 acres or more each. The largest is Red Lake, and Lake Itasca is the source of the Mississippi River.

Alternative nicknames: The Gopher State, The North Star State, The Bread and Butter State

Mississippi — The Magnolia State
This nickname honors both the state tree and flower, the magnolia, which grows virtually all over the state.

Alternative nicknames: None

Missouri — The Show Me State
This unusual nickname is usually traced back to a speech by Congressman Willard Duncan Vandiver in 1899. Speaking in Philadelphia, Vandiver said, ". . . frothy eloquence neither convinces nor satisfies me. I am from Missouri. You have got to show me."

Alternative nicknames: The Gateway to the West

Montana — The Treasure State
The vast mountains which gave this state its name also led early travelers, as they admired the sun glistening on the snow-capped peaks, to speculate as to the wealth those mountains might contain. Indeed, these mountains did contain a wealth of gold and silver.

Alternative nicknames: Land of Shining Mountains

Nebraska — The Cornhusker State
This nickname comes from the state's leading crop, corn, and the annual corn-husking (stripping off of the green protective leaves) contests that were once held in the rural towns each fall.

Alternative nicknames: The Tree Planters State

Nevada — The Silver State
Vast amounts of silver were once taken from the state's many mines. The discovery of both silver and gold in the 1860s brought thousands of miners to the area — including a young Samuel Clemens, later better known as Mark Twain.

Alternative nicknames: The Sagebrush State, Battle Born State

New Hampshire — The Granite State
Although the largest granite deposits are in quarries in Hillsboro and Merrimack Counties, mining is of little importance to New Hampshire's present-day economy. Nonetheless, in the past New Hampshire supplied granite for the Library of Congress building in Washington, D.C., and furnished the cornerstone of the United Nations Building in New York City.

Alternative nicknames: None

New Jersey — The Garden State
With its many truck farms, orchards, and flower gardens, New Jersey supplies New York City and the huge metropolitan areas near it. In fact, in 1999 the value of all agricultural goods from New Jersey topped $56 billion.

Alternative nicknames: Cockpit of the Revolution

New Mexico — Land of Enchantment
New Mexico is a region of scenic beauty and rich history. Thousands of tourists flock to New Mexico for sight-seeing, hunting, fishing, and skiing. Still standing are the ruins of an 800-room apartment house built by Indians hundreds of years before Columbus arrived in America. New Mexico has the United State's oldest road, the El Camino Real, and it has the oldest seat of government, Santa Fe, which has been a capital since 1610.

Alternative nicknames: None

New York — The Empire State
When George Washington visited the state in 1783, he predicted that it might become the seat of a new empire. New York has fulfilled its promise by becoming a leading center of transportation, communication, banking, and finance. New York is far ahead of all other states in foreign and wholesale trade.

Alternative nicknames: Excelsior State

North Carolina — The Tarheel State
During the Civil War 11 battles and 73 skirmishes were fought on North Carolina soil. During one fierce battle, some Confederate troops retreated, leaving North Carolina's forces to fight alone. Afterward, the soldiers from North Carolina allegedly threatened to put tar on the heels of the other troops so they would "stick better in the next fight."

Alternative nicknames: The Rip Van Winkle State, The Old North State

North Dakota — The Peace Garden State
The International Peace Garden is a park which lies partly in North Dakota near Bottineau and partly in Manitoba. It represents the long friendship between the U.S. and Canada.

Alternative nicknames: The Flickertail State, The Sioux State, Land of the Dakotas

Ohio — The Buckeye State
Buckeye, or horse chestnut, trees once grew plentifully on Ohio's hills and plains. Pioneers cut down many buckeye trees since they were wellsuited for building log cabins.

Alternative nicknames: Gateway State

Oklahoma — The Sooner State
The federal government first opened Oklahoma to white settlement during the late 1880s. Some settlers were so anxious to stake out claims, they arrived "sooner" than the land was opened. Authorities declared 1.9 million acres in central Oklahoma open at noon on April 22, 1889, when a pistol shot signaled the official opening. Fifty thousand people had moved in by that evening! Guthrie and Oklahoma City became cities of 10,000 persons each in a single day!

Alternative nicknames: Boomer State

Oregon — The Beaver State
During fur-trading days, Oregon supplied thousands of beaver pelts. There are more beavers in the U.S. and Canada than anywhere else in the world. Because beaver fur is soft, shiny, and wears well, cloth manufacturers were eager to use it to make fur coats or to trim collars and cuffs of cloth coats. There came to be such a demand for pelts that the beaver was the most hunted animal in North America from the 1600s through the 1800s.

Alternative nicknames: Pacific Wonderland

Pennsylvania — The Keystone State
Since Pennsylvania itself is the center of the "arch" formed by the original 13 states, it can be thought to serve as the "keystone," which is literally a wedge-shaped stone of an arch that locks and unites the other stones together. Historically, of course, Pennsylvania served as a uniting keystone by being the site of the signings of both the Declaration of Independence and the Constitution.

Alternative nicknames: Quaker State

Rhode Island — The Ocean State
The scenic 40-mile southern border of Rhode Island is located along the Atlantic Ocean. It attracts many visitors, and well-known summer resorts have developed along it as well as Narragansett Bay which extends for 28 miles inland.

Alternative nicknames: Little Rhody

South Carolina — The Palmetto State
South Carolina may have earned its nickname as a result of events during the Revolutionary War. In 1776, colonists in a small fort built of palmetto logs defeated a British fleet that tried to capture Charleston Harbor. The next day colonial commander William Moultrie saw a column of smoke rising from a burning British ship. The shape of the smoke reminded Moultrie of the palmetto. Others say that the palmetto logs of

the fort so effectively withstood British cannon fire by entrapping the cannon balls, that the palmetto gained the honor of nicknaming South Carolina by this feat.

Alternative nicknames: The Rice State, The Swamp State

South Dakota — The Coyote State

Although the coyote, also South Dakota's state animal, has nowadays spread its range virtually across the North American continent, earlier in our nation's history it was more concentrated on the Plains.

Alternative nicknames: The Sunshine State

Tennessee — The Volunteer State

Tennessee really earned its nickname, owing to its outstanding military traditions. This was first evident in the War of 1812 when large numbers of Tennesseans volunteered for service, and leaders such as Andrew Jackson distinguished themselves. Because such large numbers volunteered for the Mexican War, it was at that time that the nickname "The Volunteer State" was coined.

In the Civil War it was a state divided, with most volunteers supporting the Confederate cause, but a Unionist sentiment was evident in East Tennessee. There were 454 battles or skirmishes within the state, and Tennessee furnished more troops than any other southern state: 115,000 Confederate and 30,000 Union.

Alternative nicknames: Big Bend State

Texas — The Lone Star State

The single star on the Texas state flag gives the state its nickname, but this star recalls the 10 years Texas "stood alone" as a republic — until December 29, 1845.

Alternative nicknames: None

Utah — The Beehive State

Mormon pioneers lead by Brigham Young settled the Utah region in 1847. Their name for the area, "Deseret," means "honeybee" and was meant to stand for hard work and industry, qualities the Mormons wished to emulate.

Alternative nicknames: None

Vermont — The Green Mountain State

The famous tree-covered peaks of the Green Mountains run the entire length of central Vermont, dividing the state into eastern and western sections. It is the beauty of the Green Mountains that attracts thousands of skiers and tourists annually, making Vermont one of our most scenic states.

Alternative nicknames: None

Virginia — The Old Dominion State

This nickname was given to Virginia by King Charles II of England because Virginia remained loyal to the crown during the English Civil War of the mid-1600s when the King and the Parliament went to war over issues of religion and authority.

Alternative nicknames: Mother of Presidents, Mother of States

Washington — The Evergreen State

Washington has large areas of thick forests — firs, hemlocks, pines, and other evergreens — especially on the western slopes of the Cascade Mountains. The nickname also suggests the lush green lowlands of western Washington.

Alternative nicknames: None

West Virginia — The Mountain State

West Virginia has no large areas of level ground, except for strips of valley land along larger rivers. Mountain chains cover the entire eastern section, and steep hills and narrow valleys make up the region west of the mountains. The extreme ruggedness of the land gives it this nickname.

Alternative nicknames: None

Wisconsin — The Badger State

In addition to being home to badgers themselves, Wisconsin has a nickname that was first applied in the 1820s to the state's lead miners. As some of them lived in caves they dug right out of the hillsides, they reminded people of the badgers, burrowing similar holes.

Alternative nicknames: America's Dairyland

Wyoming — The Equality State

Wyoming women were not only the first in the nation to gain the right to vote, but also the first to hold public office and serve on juries. Esther H. Morris became the United States' first female justice of the peace in 1870, and in 1924 Mrs. Nellie Taylor Ross was elected by Wyoming voters as the first woman governor.

Alternative nicknames: None

State Tree

Alabama — Southern Pine
Alaska — Sitka Spruce
Arizona — Paloverde
Arkansas — Southern Pine
California — California Redwood
Colorado — Blue Spruce
Connecticut — White Oak
Delaware — American Holly
Florida — Sabal Palm
Georgia — Live Oak
Hawaii — Kukui
Idaho — Western White Pine
Illinois — White Oak
Indiana — Tulip Tree
Iowa — Oak
Kansas — Cottonwood
Kentucky — Kentucky Coffee Tree
Louisiana — Bald Cypress
Maine — Eastern White Pine
Maryland — White Oak
Massachusetts — American Elm
Michigan — Eastern White Pine
Minnesota — Norway Pine
Mississippi — Magnolia
Missouri — Flowering Dogwood

Montana — Ponderosa Pine
Nebraska — Cottonwood
Nevada — Single-leaf Piñon
New Hampshire — White Birch
New Jersey — Red Oak
New Mexico — Piñon Pine
New York — Sugar Maple
North Carolina — Pine
North Dakota — American Elm
Ohio — Buckeye
Oklahoma — Redbud
Oregon — Douglas Fir
Pennsylvania — Hemlock
Rhode Island — Red Maple
South Carolina — Palmetto
South Dakota — Black Hills Spruce
Tennessee — Tulip Poplar
Texas — Pecan
Utah — Blue Spruce
Vermont — Sugar Maple
Virginia — Flowering Dogwood
Washington — Western Hemlock
West Virginia — Sugar Maple
Wisconsin — Sugar Maple
Wyoming — Cottonwood

To Learn More . . .

Alabama — Southern Pine — Pine Family
The southern pine, or yellow pine, is a group of hard pines including the loblolly, longleaf, and slash pines. They are tall trees, often 100 feet high, with long needles and large cones. They are important timber trees, producing strong, tight-grained lumber for construction.

Alaska — Sitka Spruce — Pine Family
The stika spruce is a large spruce that grows along the coast of the Pacific Northwest, from northern California to southern Alaska. It has short, flattened needles and small, papery cones. It grows up to 200 feet tall and is an important source of timber.

Arizona — Paloverde — Legume Family
Paloverde trees are small trees, only growing up to 25 feet high, of the desert southwest. They have small oval leaves, yellow blossoms, and spiny twigs. The bean-like seeds grow in pods.

Arkansas — Pine — Pine Family
See Alabama.

California — California Redwood — Redwood Family
The California redwood is one of the tallest species of tree in the world, growing over 350 feet tall. It has short, flat needles and small cones. The bark of the redwood is very resistant to fire. It is a very important timber tree, though found only along the coast of northern California and southern Oregon.

Colorado — Blue Spruce — Pine Family
The blue spruce grows on mountain slopes in the southern Rockies. It has short, silver-blue needles and papery cones. It has been planted as an ornamental and yard tree throughout the northern U.S.

Connecticut — White Oak — Beech Family

The white oak is one of the most common oaks in the eastern half of the U.S. It is deciduous and grows to 100 feet in height. The leaves are 5 to 9 inches long, with rounded lobes. It bears sweet acorns. Its wood is very popular for furniture, flooring, and paneling.

Delaware — American Holly — Holly Family

The American holly is a shrub or tree that grows along the Atlantic seaboard and in the southeast. It has spine-fringed, evergreen leaves and characteristic red berries in the winter. The holly's evergreen leaves and red berries, bright in midwinter, are often associated with Christmas, the time of light in darkness, of new life in the midst of death.

Florida — Sabal Palm — Palm Family

The sabal palm, or cabbage palmetto, is a tall palm with large, 6-foot, fan-shaped leaves. It has small white flowers and small black fruit. The people of Jerusalem strewed Jesus' path with palms to honor Him as a king and therefore the Church uses palms as sacramentals on Passion, or Palm, Sunday.

Georgia — Live Oak — Beech Family

The live oak is an oak of the southern coastal regions. It has medium-sized, oval evergreen leaves. The acorns of the live oak, unlike most red oaks, are not bitter. The tree grows to a height of 50 feet, but the crown can spread out 100 feet in diameter, sometimes with limbs resting on the ground. In swampy areas the limbs are often festooned with Spanish moss and ferns.

Hawaii – Kukui

The Kukui is a medium-sized tree native to the tropical Pacific. The small white flowers grow in clusters close to the branches. Oil from its nut is used for lighting as well as medicinal purposes.

Idaho — Western White Pine — Pine Family

The western white pine is a close relative of the eastern white pine which is the state tree of Maine. It grows in the northwestern states of our country. Growing up to 175 feet in height, the western white pine has 3- to 5-inch long needles, and long, narrow cones, typically 5 to 15 inches in length.

Illinois — White Oak — Beech Family
See Connecticut.

Indiana — Tulip Tree — Magnolia Family

The tulip tree — also called the tulip poplar, which is Tennessee's state tree, and the yellow poplar — is a tall tree of the eastern forests. It has leaves with 4 lobes and fairly large blossoms with yellow-green petals, tipped with orange at the base.

Iowa — Oak — Beech Family
See Connecticut.

Kansas — Cottonwood — Willow Family

The prairie cottonwood is the most common cottonwood in Kansas. Cottonwoods are large trees with serrated, heart-shaped leaves. Their name is derived from the cottony tufts which help to broadcast the tree's seeds. Prairie cottonwoods grow mostly along rivers and streams.

Kentucky — Kentucky Coffee Tree — Legume Family

The Kentucky coffee tree is a large tree of the Ohio Valley. It has compound leaves with small, pointed-oval leaflets. Its flowers are small and greenish-white.

Louisiana — Bald Cypress — Redwood Family

The bald cypress is a large tree of southern swamps. It has short, deciduous needles that turn yellow-brown before falling. It produces nearly round cones, about 1 inch in diameter. The most characteristic feature of this tree is the development of cypress "knees," which are columns protruding upward from the roots, often rising from the water.

Maine — Eastern White Pine — Pine Family

The eastern white pine is the largest conifer found in the northeastern corner of the U.S. It has medium length, soft needles and 4- to 8-inch cones. At one time the white pine was among the most important timber trees in the nation.

Maryland — White Oak — Beech Family
See Connecticut.

Massachusetts — American Elm — Elm Family

The American elm has been a popular tree of yards and parks in the eastern half of the U.S. It is a fairly tall tree with pointed, serrated, elliptical leaves. The seeds develop in small wafers shaped somewhat like rolled oatmeal. Many American elms have died in the last decades due to Dutch elm disease.

Michigan — Eastern White Pine — Pine Family
See Maine.

Minnesota — Norway Pine — Pine Family
The Norway pine, also known as the red pine, is a fairly tall pine of the northeastern states. It has long needles and fairly small 1- to 2-inch cones. It is an important timber tree.

Mississippi — Magnolia — Magnolia Family
The magnolia is a striking tree of the south-eastern states. It grows to 80 feet in height, particularly near water. The evergreen leaves are glossy, leathery, and large — up to 10 inches. The blossoms, which bloom in spring and early summer, are fragrant, with creamy-white petals. These memorable flowers can be very large, growing up to nine inches in diameter.

Missouri — Flowering Dogwood — Dogwood Family
The flowering dogwood is a small tree of the eastern U.S. It has oval, deciduous leaves and showy flower clusters. The flower clusters consist of small, greenish-white flowers surrounded by large white bracts, which many people assume are petals. The seeds are in small, bright-red fruit.

Montana — Ponderosa Pine — Pine Family
The ponderosa pine is a very tall pine of the western mountainous regions. The needles grow up to 10 inches long, and the pine cones are oval. The ponderosa pine is an important timber tree.

Nebraska — Cottonwood — Willow Family
See Kansas.

Nevada — Single-leaf Piñon — Pine Family
The single-leaf piñon is the northernmost of the 4 species of piñon. Piñons are small trees with short needles and small, round cones with edible seeds. The piñon is common in semi-arid regions of the Southwest.

New Hampshire — White Birch — Birch Family
The white birth, or paper birch, is found across the northern tier of states. It is a medium-sized tree with rounded leaves. Its most characteristic feature is its bright white bark which peels off in layers. From this bark woodland Indians made their canoes, in which the early French missionaries traveled to evangelize.

New Jersey — Red Oak — Beech Family
The northern red oak is the most common member of the red oak group. It is a medium-sized tree with tough wood. The leaves have pointed lobes and turn deep red in the fall. Acorns are oval in shape.

New Mexico — Piñon — Pine Family
The piñon is a small pine of the southwestern semi-arid regions. It has short leaves and small cones with edible seeds.

New York — Sugar Maple — Maple Family
The sugar maple is a valued hardwood of the northeast. The leaves have 5 pointed lobes and turn bright yellow to red in the fall. Seeds have a wing which enables them to "helicopter" down to the ground. The sugar maple wood is very hard and is used in furniture, bowling alleys, and butcher blocks. In spring the trees are tapped for sap which is boiled down to make maple syrup and sugar.

North Carolina — Southern Pine — Pine Family
See Alabama.

North Dakota — American Elm — Elm Family
See Massachusetts.

Ohio — Buckeye — Horse Chestnut Family
The buckeye is a medium-sized tree of the Ohio and Mississippi valley. The leaves are compound, with 5 tapered leaflets radiating from a central point. The seeds are large, from 1 to 2 inches in diameter, and are covered in a spiny, leathery skin which splits open in late fall.

Oklahoma — Redbud — Legume Family
The redbud is a small tree of the eastern U.S. The small, pink to lavender flowers grow close to the branches and bloom in early spring, before leaves appear. The leaves are heart-shaped and turn yellow to orange in fall. Seeds grow in brown pods shaped like pea pods.

Oregon — Douglas Fir — Pine Family
The Douglas fir is a tall tree — often growing to 250 feet in height — of the western mountain regions. It has short needles and medium-sized cones. It is an important timber tree and is also frequently used as a Christmas tree.

Pennsylvania — Hemlock — Pine Family

The hemlock is a small to medium-sized tree of the northeastern states. It has short, flat, soft needles that grow on 2 sides of the branches. The cones are small and oval in shape.

Rhode Island — Red Maple — Maple Family

The red maple is a medium-sized tree of the eastern U.S. It has 3 triangular leaves with saw-toothed edges, that turn bright red in the fall. The seeds have wings attached which allow the wind to blow them around the woods.

South Carolina — Palmetto — Palm Family

See Florida.

South Dakota — Black Hills Spruce — Pine Family

Most white spruce trees grow in Canada, with the range extending into Minnesota, Wisconsin, Michigan, New York, Vermont, New Hampshire, and Maine. In The Black Hills of South Dakota, however, a population of white spruces grows in isolation from the main range. These trees are known locally as Black Hills spruce. This tree grows up to 75 feet tall, has 1-inch needles, and 1- to 2-inch cones.

Tennessee — Tulip Poplar — Magnolia Family

The tulip tree — also called the tulip tree, which is Indiana's state tree, and the yellow poplar — is a tall tree of the eastern forests. It has leaves with 4 lobes and fairly large blossoms with yellow-green petals, tipped with orange at the base.

Texas — Pecan — Walnut Family

The pecan is a hickory, and like other hickories, has compound leaves with 9 to 17 leaflets. It grows to 140 feet in height. Unlike other hickories, pecan wood is not particularly strong. The most important commercial feature of the pecan is the nut. In the native tree, the nut is about 1 inch long, with a thin shell. Cultivated varieties have nuts up to 3 inches long. Pecan nuts are an important crop in many parts of the South.

Utah — Blue Spruce — Pine Family

See Colorado.

Vermont — Sugar Maple — Maple Family

See New York.

Virginia — Flowering Dogwood — Dogwood Family

See Missouri.

Washington — Western Hemlock — Pine Family

The western hemlock is the tallest of the North American hemlocks, growing up to 175 feet tall. It has small cones and short, soft needles growing on 2 sides of the branches.

West Virginia — Sugar Maple — Maple Family

See New York.

Wisconsin — Sugar Maple — Maple Family

See New York.

Wyoming — Cottonwood — Willow Family

See Kansas.

Trees

I think that I shall never see
A poem lovely as a tree.

A tree whose hungry mouth is prest
Against the earth's sweet flowing breast;

A tree that looks at God all day,
And lifts her leafy arms to pray;

A tree that may in Summer wear
A nest of robins in her hair;

Upon whose bosom snow has lain;
Who intimately lives with rain.

Poems are made by fools like me,
But only God can make a tree.

— **Joyce Kilmer**
American poet and Catholic convert

Famous Native

Alabama — Helen Keller	Montana — Gary Cooper
Alaska — Edgar Nollner	Nebraska — Gerald Ford
Arizona — Geronimo	Nevada — Wovoka (Jack Wilson)
Arkansas — Douglas MacArthur	New Hampshire — Alan Shepard, Jr.
California — Richard Nixon	New Jersey — James Fenimore Cooper
Colorado — Jack Dempsey	New Mexico — Maria Martinez
Connecticut — Harriet Beecher Stowe	New York — Theodore Roosevelt
Delaware — Pierre Du Pont	North Carolina — Virginia Dare
Florida — Sidney Poitier	North Dakota — Lawrence Welk
Georgia — Martin Luther King, Jr.	Ohio — Thomas Edison
Hawaii — King Kamehameha	Oklahoma — Will Rogers
Idaho — Ezra Pound	Oregon — Chief Joseph
Illinois — Archbishop Fulton J. Sheen	Pennsylvania — Daniel Boone
Indiana — Wilbur Wright	Rhode Island — Gilbert Charles Stuart
Iowa — Herbert Hoover	South Carolina — Andrew Jackson
Kansas — Amelia Earhart	South Dakota — Hubert Humphrey
Kentucky — Abraham Lincoln	Tennessee — Davy Crockett
Louisiana — Louis Armstrong	Texas — Dwight Eisenhower
Maine — Henry Wadsworth Longfellow	Utah — Loretta Young
Maryland — Francis Scott Key	Vermont — Calvin Coolidge
Massachusetts — Clara Barton	Virginia — Lewis & Clark
Michigan — Henry Ford	Washington — Bing Crosby
Minnesota — Judy Garland	West Virginia — Chuck Yeager
Mississippi — William Faulkner	Wisconsin — Frank Lloyd Wright
Missouri — Jesse James	Wyoming — Jackson Pollack

To Learn More . . .

Alabama — Helen Keller (1880-1968)
Helen Keller became blind and deaf from a fever at 19 months. She was taught to communicate and read by Anna Sullivan and went on to graduate with honors from Radcliffe College. She then became a famous author, speaker, and advocate for the handicapped.
Other famous natives: George Wallace, politician; Coretta Scott King, Civil Rights activist; Nat "King" Cole, singer; Hank Williams, singer; Tallulah Bankhead, actress; Harper Lee, author; Jesse Owens, Olympic runner; Joe Louis, boxer; Satchel Paige, baseball player; Willie Mays, baseball player; Hank Aaron, baseball player; Walker Percy, Catholic novelist.

Alaska — Edgar Nollner (1904?-1999)
In 1925 the city of Nome, Alaska, was struck by a diphtheria epidemic, but the only medicine available was in Nenana, about 700 miles away. The only way to bring the medicine to Nome was by dog sled. Edgar Nollner was one of the heroic "mushers" who used a relay of dog sleds to bring in the medicine which stemmed the epidemic.

Arizona — Geronimo (1829-1909)
Geronimo was a chief of the Chiricahua Apaches. His Apache name was Goyaale, but the Mexicans gave him the name "Geronimo." During the 1870s and 1880s, Geronimo led his warriors in a series of raids and battles against settlers and the U.S. Army. He finally settled in Oklahoma in 1894 where he lived the rest of his life.
Other famous natives: Barry Goldwater, politician; Cochise, Indian chief; Cesar Chavez, Civil Rights activist; Marty Robbins, singer.

28

Arkansas — Douglas MacArthur (1880-1964)
The son of a famous general, Douglas MacArthur graduated from West Point at the top of his class in 1903. He rose through the ranks until 1919 when he was appointed superintendent of the Military Academy. In 1930 he was named Army Chief of Staff and in 1935 was appointed military advisor to the Philippine government. After the Japanese attack, he became commander of all army forces in the Pacific and received the Japanese surrender in 1945.
Other famous natives: Bill Clinton, president; Eldridge Cleaver, Civil Rights activist; Johnny Cash, singer; Glen Campbell, singer; Dick Powell, actor; Alan Ladd, actor; "Dizzy" Dean, baseball player.

California — Richard Nixon (1913-1994)
Richard Nixon was elected to the House of Representatives in 1946, the Senate in 1950; he served as vice president under Dwight Eisenhower and eventually won the presidency in 1968 and reelection in 1972. Due to the Watergate scandal, he resigned the presidency in 1974.
Other famous natives: Earl Warren, Chief Justice; John Steinbeck, author; Ernest and Julio Gallo, vintners; William Randolph Hearst, publisher; Jack London, author; Robert Frost, poet; Shirley Temple, actress; Gregory Peck, actor; Joe DiMaggio, baseball player.

Colorado — Jack Dempsey (1895-1983)
Jack Dempsey started boxing in mining camps and went on to become one of the most popular boxers of all time. He won the heavy-weight championship in 1919 and held the title for 7 years before he lost it to Gene Tunney.
Other famous natives: Lon Chaney, actor; Douglas Fairbanks, actor.

Connecticut — Harriet Beecher Stowe (1811-1896)
Harriet Beecher Stowe was an author of several novels about New England life, but she is best known for *Uncle Tom's Cabin*, an anti-slavery novel which intensified opposition to slavery in the North during the years leading up to the Civil War.
Other famous natives: George Bush, 43rd president; Benedict Arnold, Revolutionary War leader; Nathan Hale, Revolutionary War patriot; John Brown, abolitionist; Noah Webster, lexicographer; Charles Goodyear, inventor; Samuel Colt, inventor; P. T. Barnum, entertainer; J.P. Morgan, financier; Katharine Hepburn, actress; Robert Mitchum, actor.

Delaware — Pierre S. Du Pont (1870-1954)
Pierre Du Pont inherited the Du Pont chemical company and served as president of the company from 1915 to 1919 and chairman of the Board from 1919-1940.
Other famous natives: Howard Pyle, illustrator.

Florida — Sidney Poitier (born 1927)
He first appeared as an actor on Broadway in 1948 and then went on to act in films starting in 1950. His best known films include *Raisin in the Sun* and *In the Heat of the Night*. He won an Academy Award for *Lilies of the Field*.
Other famous natives: Pat Boone, singer; Ben Vereen, dancer; Chris Evert, tennis player.

Georgia — Martin Luther King, Jr. (1929-1968)
Dr. King was a Baptist minister and became active in the Civil Rights movement in the 1950s. He employed passive resistance in boycotts and marches in the 1960s. He was assassinated in Memphis in 1968.
Other famous natives: Jimmy Carter, president; Osceola, Indian chief; Sidney Lanier, author; Joel Chandler Harris, author; Flannery O'Connor, author; Margaret Mitchell, author; Oliver Hardy, actor; Ray Charles, singer; Ty Cobb, baseball player; Jackie Robinson, baseball player.

Hawaii — King Kamehameha (1737?-1819)
King Kamehameha became a chief in 1781 and by 1795 had conquered most of the islands of Hawaii and made himself king. By 1810 he ruled all the Hawaiian islands.
Other famous natives: Queen Liliuokalani, ruler.

Idaho — Ezra Pound (1885-1972)
After attending the University of Pennsylvania and teaching briefly, Ezra Pound left the U.S. for Europe and began to write poetry. Although his own poetry is highly regarded, he has been equally esteemed as a critic and an influence on other writers, particularly W. B. Yeats and T. S. Eliot.
Other famous natives: Gutzon Borghum, sculptor; Harmon Killebrew, baseball player.

Illinois — Archbishop Fulton J. Sheen (1895-1979)
In 1926 Fulton J. Sheen began teaching at the Catholic University of America and also published his first book. He went on to write over 50 books and gave radio talks beginning in 1930. During the 1950s he had one of the most popular television programs, "Life is Worth Living."
Other famous natives: Ronald Reagan, president; William Jennings Bryan, Chief Justice; Jane

Addams, human rights activist; Charles W. Post, cereal manufacturer; Finley Peter Dunne, Catholic journalist; Edgar Rice Burroughs, author; John Dos Passos, author; Ernest Hemingway, author; Carl Sandburg, poet; Jack Benny, entertainer; Bob Newhart, entertainer; William Holden, actor; Charlton Heston, actor.

Indiana — Wilbur Wright (1867-1912)

Along with his brother Orville, Wilbur Wright began to make bicycles in 1892. The brothers later became interested in flight and began to design gliders. They began designing a powered airplane in 1902 and in 1903 it flew successfully.

Other famous natives: Benjamin Harrison, president; Ambrose Burnside, Civil War general; James Whitcomb Riley, poet; Theodore Dreiser, author; Kurt Vonnegut, author; Cole Porter, composer; Hoagy Carmichael, composer; Red Skelton, entertainer; Larry Bird, basketball player.

Iowa — Herbert Hoover (1874-1964)

Herbert Hoover was an engineer and a businessman before he entered government service during the Wilson administration. He was elected president in 1928. Seven months after he took the oath of office, the stock market crashed, initiating the Great Depression. Because of his perceived ineffectiveness in dealing with the economic crisis, he lost his bid for reelection in 1932.

Other famous natives: John L. Lewis, human rights activist; Glenn Miller, musician; Grant Wood, artist; "Buffalo" Bill Cody, entertainer; John Wayne, actor.

Kansas — Amelia Earhart (1897-1937?)

Amelia Earhart was the first woman to fly across the Atlantic Ocean alone and the first to cross the U.S. alone. In 1937 she began an attempt to fly around the world, but her plane vanished in the Pacific Ocean near Howland Island.

Other famous natives: Robert Dole, politician; Buster Keaton, actor; Vivian Vance, actress; James Naismith, inventor of basketball.

Kentucky — Abraham Lincoln (1809-1865)

Abraham Lincoln's first elected office was the Illinois General Assembly, to which he was elected in 1834. He was elected to the U.S. House of Representatives in 1846. In 1860, as the candidate for the newly formed Republican party, he was elected U.S. president. His election triggered the secession of the southern states, which led to the Civil War. He served as president throughout the Civil War. At virtually the same time the Civil War was ending, he was assassinated by John Wilkes Booth.

Other famous natives: Jefferson Davis, Confederate president; Kit Carson, frontiersman; Carrie Nation, temperance leader; Robert Penn Warren, poet and novelist; D.W. Griffith, director; Loretta Lynn, singer; Muhammad Ali, boxer.

Louisiana — Louis Armstrong (1900-1971)

Louis Armstrong began to play the coronet in jazz bands as a teenager. He had a successful performing and recording career from 1922 virtually to his death. He was known for brilliant tone and technique, his gruff singing voice, and for being the first musician to sing scat.

Other famous natives: Pierre Beauregard, general; Huey Long, politician; Jelly-Roll Morton, musician.

Maine — Henry Wadsworth Longfellow (1807-1882)

Longfellow was the most popular American poet of the 19th century, although 20th century critics do not value him so highly. His best known works are "Evangeline," "The Song of Hiawatha," "The Village Blacksmith," and "Paul Revere's Ride."

Other famous natives: Nelson Rockefeller, politician; Edwin Arlington Robinson, poet; Edna St. Vincent Millay, poet.

Maryland — Francis Scott Key (1779-1843)

Francis Scott Key was a lawyer in the District of Columbia who happened to witness the British bombardment of Fort McHenry near Baltimore during the War of 1812. As he watched the battle, he wrote "The Star Spangled Banner," which became immediately popular.

Other famous natives: Frederick Douglass, abolitionist; H. L. Mencken, journalist; Edwin Booth, actor; John Wilkes Booth, actor (President Lincoln's assassin); George Herman "Babe" Ruth, baseball player.

Massachusetts — Clara Barton (1821-1912)

Clara Barton was one of the first women to practice as a battlefield nurse, which she did in the Civil War. Having observed the war of the International Red Cross in Europe, she established the American Red Cross in 1881.

Other famous natives: John Adams, president; John Quincy Adams, president; John F. Kennedy, president; George Bush, 41st president; Benjamin Franklin, statesman and scientist; Samuel Adams, Revolutionary War leader; Paul Revere, Revolutionary War figure; Nathaniel Hawthorne, author; Ralph Waldo Emerson, author; Henry David Thoreau, author; Edgar Allan Poe, author;

John Greenleaf Whittier, poet; James Russell Lowell, poet; Emily Dickinson, poet; Eli Whitney, inventor; Henry Adams, author; W. E. B. DuBois, Civil Rights activist; Leonard Bernstein, conductor; Winslow Homer, artist; Samuel Morse, inventor; Jack Haley, actor; Ray Bolger, actor; Rocky Marciano, boxer.

Michigan — Henry Ford (1863-1947)

Henry Ford built his first automobile in 1896 and organized the Ford Motor Company in 1903. He was the first American automaker to employ the assembly-line methods, and he was the first to offer a low-priced automobile.

Other famous natives: Jim and Will Kellogg, inventors; Charles Lindbergh, aviator; James Hoffa, labor leader; Ring Lardner, author; Edna Ferber, author; Danny Thomas, actor; Stevie Wonder, singer; Francis Ford Coppola, director; "Sugar" Ray Robinson, boxer.

Minnesota — Judy Garland (1922-1969)

Born Frances Gumm, Judy Garland made her stage debut at the age of 5. She made her first film when she was 14 years old and made 34 films in all. Her best-known role was as Dorothy in *The Wizard of Oz*.

Other famous natives: Eugene McCarthy, politician; Sinclair Lewis, author; J. Paul Getty, oil tycoon; Richard W. Sears, businessman; F. Scott Fitzgerald, author; Charles Schulz, cartoonist; Wanda Gag, author.

Mississippi — William Faulkner (1897-1962)

William Faulkner was one of the most important American novelists of the 20th century. Most of his fiction centers around the mythical Yoknapatawpha County and its inhabitants. He was awarded the Nobel Prize for literature in 1949.

Other famous natives: Richard Wright, author; Eudora Welty, author; Tennessee Williams, playwright; Shelby Foote, author; Leontyne Price, opera singer; B. B. King, musician; Elvis Presley, singer.

Missouri — Jesse James (1847-1882)

While still a teenager, Jesse James served the Confederate cause with Quantrill's raiders and was consequently outlawed at the end of the Civil War. He and his gang, including his brother Frank, engaged in a 16-year crime spree throughout the Midwest. He was finally killed by former members of his own gang.

Other famous natives: Harry S. Truman, president; George Washington Carver, inventor; J. C. Penney, businessman; Walter Cronkite, news commentator; Mark Twain, author; T. S. Eliot, poet; Langston Hughes, poet; Vincent Price, actor; Chuck Berry, musician; "Casey" Stengel, baseball player; Yogi Berra, baseball player.

Montana — Gary Cooper (1901-1961)

Born Frank James Cooper in Helena, Montana, Gary Cooper became a very popular actor particularly in western movies. His first major role was in *The Virginian* in 1929, and later films included *A Farewell to Arms, Meet John Doe*, and *Mr. Deeds Goes to Town*. He won Academy Awards for his roles in *Sergeant York* and *High Noon*. Near the end of his life, he was received into the Catholic Church.

Other famous natives: Myrna Loy, actress.

Nebraska — Gerald Ford (born 1913)

Gerald Ford served in the Navy during World War II. In 1948 he was elected to the House of Representatives where he served 13 terms, eventually becoming House Minority Leader in 1965. He became vice president in 1973 upon the resignation of Spiro Agnew. In 1974 Richard Nixon resigned the presidency and thereon Ford became president. He lost his bid for reelection to Jimmy Carter in 1976.

Other famous natives: Red Cloud, Indian chief; Fred Astaire, dancer; Harold Lloyd, actor; Henry Fonda, actor.

Nevada — Wovoka (1856?-1932)

Wovoka was a Paiute Indian who was adopted as a boy by a white man named David Wilson, and so is sometimes known as Jack Wilson. After an illness in 1889, he established a new, messianic sect among the Plains Indians, calling it the Ghost Dance religion. His teaching was that if the Indians would perform certain ritual songs and dances and live in peace among themselves, then all earthly problems would cease, the buffalo would return, and the ancestors of the Indians would return to life.

New Hampshire — Alan B. Shepard, Jr. (1923-1998)

Alan Shepard, Jr., served in the Navy during World War II, after which he became a Navy test pilot. In 1959 he was selected for the astronaut program, and in 1961 he became the first American in space as he was rocketed from Cape Canaveral in Freedom 7. He went 117 miles above the earth and landed in the Atlantic Ocean. In 1971 he led Apollo 14 to the third moon landing.

Other famous natives: Franklin Pierce, president;

Mary Baker Eddy, founder of Christian Scientist sect; Horace Greeley, newspaper editor.

New Jersey — James Fenimore Cooper (1789-1851)

James Fenimore Cooper originally intended to become a farmer and settled in upstate New York. He was reading a novel out loud to his wife one day, and he declared that he could write one that was better. His wife challenged him to do so and he began to write. His first successful novel was *The Spy*, published in 1821. His best-known works are the *Leather-stocking Tales*, 5 novels which center around the character of the frontiersman Natty Bumppo.

Other famous natives: Grover Cleveland, president; Aaron Burr, vice president; Stephen Crane, author; Joyce Kilmer, Catholic poet; Charles Addams, cartoonist; Paul Robeson, singer; Frank Sinatra, singer; "Count" Basie, musician; Jack Nicholson, actor; Jerry Lewis, entertainer.

New Mexico — Maria Martinez (1887?-1980)

Maria Martinez learned how to make pots from her aunt in the San Ildefonso pueblo, north of Santa Fe. She is largely responsible for the revival of pottery-making in the pueblos of New Mexico. Her characteristic black-on-black ware, crafted in collaboration with her husband, Julian, has achieved worldwide fame for its artistry.

Other famous natives: Bill Mauldin, editorial cartoonist.

New York — Theodore Roosevelt (1858-1919)

Born into a wealthy and prominent family, Theodore Roosevelt entered politics after graduating from Harvard in 1880, serving 3 terms in the New York State Assembly. He retired temporarily from politics in 1884 and ranched in the Dakota Territory. In 1898 he led a troop of cavalry volunteers in Cuba during the Spanish-American War. He was elected vice president in 1900 and became president when President McKinley was assassinated in 1901. Roosevelt was elected in his own right in 1905. His presidency is most closely associated with efforts to break business monopolies and with the conservation of natural resources.

Other famous natives: Martin Van Buren, president; Millard Fillmore, president; Franklin Delano Roosevelt, president; John Jay, Chief Justice; Washington Irving, author; Walt Whitman, poet; Herman Melville, author; William F. Buckley, Catholic journalist; George Gershwin, composer; Norman Rockwell, artist;

Julius "Groucho" Marx, entertainer; Lucille Ball, entertainer; Danny Kaye, entertainer; Humphrey Bogart, actor; James Cagney, actor; Lou Gehrig, baseball player.

North Carolina — Virginia Dare (1587-?)

Virginia Dare was born in the English settlement on Roanoke Island, becoming the first child of English parentage born in America. Her later life is unknown because of the mysterious disappearance of the colony.

Other famous natives: James Polk, president; Andrew Johnson, president; O. Henry, author; Charles Kuralt, news commentator; Earl Scruggs, musician; Andy Griffith, actor; Richard Petty, race car driver; "Meadowlark" Lemon, basketball player.

North Dakota — Lawrence Welk (1903-1989)

Lawrence Welk, orchestra and big-band leader, popularized music he termed "champagne music" for its light, bubbly character. He hosted a popular television show which ran from the late 1950s to 1975; it featured costumed performances of popular dance and show music. He was a devout Catholic.

Other famous natives: Eric Severeid, news commentator; Peggy Lee, singer; Roger Maris, baseball player.

Ohio — Thomas Edison (1847-1931)

Despite only three months of formal schooling, Thomas Edison became one of the most prolific mechanical inventors of all time, receiving 1,093 patents in his lifetime. His best-known inventions are the electric light and the phonograph.

Other famous natives: Ulysses Grant, president; Rutherford Hayes, president; James Garfield, president; Benjamin Harrison, president; William McKinley, president; William Taft, president; Warren Harding, president; William Tecumseh Sherman, general; Zane Grey, author; Hart Crane, author; James Thurber, author; Ambrose Bierce, author; Clarence Darrow, lawyer; Orville Wright, aviator; Annie Oakley, entertainer; Clark Gable, actor; Roy Rogers, entertainer; Stephen Spielberg, director; John Glenn, astronaut; Neil Armstrong, astronaut.

Oklahoma — Will Rogers (1879-1935)

Will Rogers's first job was as a cowboy, but he became famous as a humorous author, lecturer, and star of vaudeville, film, and radio. He was liked for his down-to-earth philosophy. Two of his statements became catch phrases during the 1920s and 1930s: "All I know is what I read in the papers," and "I never met a man I didn't like." He died in a plane crash off the coast of Alaska.

Other famous natives: John Berryman, poet; Ralph Ellison, author; Woody Guthrie, singer; Patti Page, singer; Jim Thorpe, Olympic athlete; Mickey Mantle, baseball player.

Oregon — Chief Joseph (1840?-1904)

Chief Joseph became a chief of the Nez Perce tribe in 1873 and refused to recognize a treaty allowing white settlement in his people's territory. He led his tribe in war against the settlers in 1876, but was forced to surrender in 1877. He is remembered for his words upon surrender, "I will fight no more forever."

Other famous natives: Linus Pauling, chemist.

Pennsylvania — Daniel Boone (1734-1820)

Daniel Boone grew up on the frontier and learned to hunt and live in the wilderness. He served in the militia during the French and Indian War, but saw little action in battle. He established the main route into the western territories via the Cumberland Gap, becoming one of the first settlers in what is now Kentucky. Eventually he moved even farther west, living the last years of his life in Missouri.

Other famous natives: James Buchanan, president; Betsy Ross, seamstress; Anthony Wayne, general; George McClellan, general; Robert Fulton, inventor; John Updike, author; Andrew Wyeth, artist; the Barrymores: Ethel, John, and Lionel, actors; W. C. Fields, entertainer; James Stewart, actor; Bill Cosby, entertainer; Tommy Dorsey, musician; Perry Como, singer; "Red" Grange, football player; Joe Namath, football player; Wallis Warfield, Duchess of Windsor; Grace Kelly, Princess of Monaco.

Rhode Island — Gilbert Charles Stuart (1755-1828)

Gilbert Stuart studied art under the well-known painter Benjamin West. He spent 10 years painting in England, but returned to the U.S. in 1792. The last few years of his career he spent as a portrait painter; his best known paintings are portraits of George Washington which he executed in 1795 and 1796.

Other famous natives: King Philip, Indian chief; Oliver Hazard Perry, general; H. P. Lovecraft, author; George M. Cohan, composer.

South Carolina — Andrew Jackson (1767-1845)

Andrew Jackson first came to prominence as a militia leader in the War of 1812 during which he defeated the British in the Battle of New Orleans

and gained the nickname "Old Hickory." He was the first candidate for the presidency to appeal deliberately to the frontiersman and common man, and he won election in 1828.

Other famous natives: John Calhoun, senator; James Longstreet, general; Eartha Kitt, entertainer; "Dizzy" Gillespie, musician.

South Dakota — Hubert Humphrey (1911-1978)

After working as a pharmacist and a teacher of political science, Hubert Humphrey entered politics in 1943, being elected mayor of Minneapolis, Minnesota, in 1945. He was elected to the U.S. Senate in 1948 and became vice president in 1964 under Lyndon Johnson. He ran for the presidency in 1968 but was defeated by Richard Nixon.

Other famous natives: George McGovern, politician; Sitting Bull, Indian chief.

Tennessee — Davy Crockett (1786-1836)

Davy Crockett's early life was rather unsettled because of his father's lack of success. Davy joined the army in 1813 and fought against the Creek Indians. He became a representative of the state of Tennessee in 1827 and served 3 terms. He moved to Texas in 1835 to better his fortunes and arrived in the middle of the Texas War for independence from Mexico. He joined the Texans at the Alamo in San Antonio where he, along with all other defenders, was killed by General Santa Anna's troops.

Other famous natives: Nathan Bedford Forrest, general; John Crowe Ransom, poet; Dolly Parton, singer.

Texas — Dwight Eisenhower (1890-1969)

Dwight Eisenhower graduated from West Point in 1915. During the 1930s he became an aid to General Douglas MacArthur who was Chief of Staff of the U.S. Army. In 1942 he was named commanding general of the American forces in Europe. In 1943 he was appointed Supreme Commander of the Allied Forces for the D-Day invasion which initiated the Allied victory in the European theater. He was nominated for the presidency in 1952 by the Republican party and won in a landslide; he was reelected in 1956.

Other famous natives: Lyndon B. Johnson, president; Audie Murphy, entertainer; Chester Nimitz, general; Dan Rather, news commentator; Katherine Anne Porter, author; Larry McMurtry, author; Larry Hagman, actor; King Vidor, director; Willie Nelson, singer; Bob Wills, singer; Kenny Rogers, singer; Babe Zaharias, Olympic athlete; A. J. Foyt, race-car driver.

Utah — Loretta Young (1913-2000)

Loretta Young was an actress who starred in over 100 films, had a series on TV that ran for 8 years, won 3 best-actress Emmys, won the Oscar for her performance in the movie, *The Farmer's Daughter*, and was nominated for one for playing the nun in the movie, *Come to the Stable*. She was a devout Catholic and an essential part in the Catholic-sponsored Family Theatre Productions for 53 years.

Other famous natives: the Osmond family singers, Donny, Marie, et. al.

Vermont — Calvin Coolidge (1872-1933)

Calvin Coolidge first came to national prominence as governor of Massachusetts (elected in 1918). He won the vice-presidential nomination of the Republican Party in 1920 as running mate to Warren G. Harding. Upon Harding's death in 1923, Vice President Coolidge was propelled into the presidency, being sworn into office by his father (a notary public), at the family farm in Vermont. Reelected once, Coolidge presided over the economic boom times of the 1920s.

Other famous natives: Chester Arthur, president; John Deere, inventor; Rudy Vallee, singer.

Virginia — William Clark and Meriwether Lewis (1770-1838 and 1774-1809)

In 1803 Lewis and Clark were appointed by Thomas Jefferson to explore the newly acquired Louisiana Purchase. They followed the Missouri River up to the Rocky Mountains and then crossed the Mountains, eventually reaching the Pacific Ocean in 1805. They returned to St. Louis in 1806, bringing much information about the western territories and having established peaceful contact with several Indian tribes.

Other famous natives: George Washington, president; Thomas Jefferson, president; James Madison, president; James Monroe, president; Zachary Taylor, president; Woodrow Wilson, president; John Marshall, Chief Justice; Patrick Henry, Revolutionary War leader; Robert E. Lee, general; Thomas "Stonewall" Jackson, general; Bill "Bojangles" Robinson, dancer; Francis X. Bushman, actor; Randolph Scott, actor; George C. Scott, actor; Roy Clark, musician; Arthur Ashe, tennis player; Fran Tarkenton, football player.

Washington — Harry "Bing" Crosby (1904-1977)

Bing Crosby, a Catholic, began his singing career in 1924 in Los Angeles and began to make movie and radio appearances in the 1930s, eventually becoming one of the most popular entertainers of the mid-20th century. His best-known song is "White Christmas," which he sang in the movie *Holiday Inn*. He won an Academy Award in 1944 for portraying a priest in *Going My Way*.

Other famous natives: Chief Seattle, Indian chief.

West Virginia — Chuck Yeager (born 1923)

Chuck Yeager served as a fighter pilot during World War II and then became a test pilot. He was the first man to fly faster than the speed of sound, which he did in the Bell X-1 Rocket plane in 1947.

Other famous natives: Pearl Buck, author; Walter Reuther, labor leader; Mary Lou Retton, Olympic athlete.

Wisconsin — Frank Lloyd Wright (1867-1959)

Frank Lloyd Wright began his architectural career in Chicago in 1887. He became the best-known American architect of the 20th century and was noted initially for his "prairie style," which emphasized horizontal forms. His later style was more curvilinear and employed cast concrete. His best-known works include the Falling Water House in Uniontown, Pennsylvania, and the Guggenheim Museum in New York City.

Other famous natives: William Renquist, Chief Justice; Robert LaFollette, politician; Joseph McCarthy, politician; Thorton Wilder, playwright; Georgia O'Keefe, artist; Orson Welles, actor; Lee Liberace, entertainer.

Wyoming — Jackson Pollack (1912-1956)

Jackson Pollack was one of the primary members of the school of abstract expressionists. He is known for "action painting" in which the paint is allowed to form its own patterns as it is dribbled and thrown onto the canvas.

State Landmark

Alabama — Tuskegee Institute
Alaska — Mount McKinley
Arizona — Grand Canyon
Arkansas — Crater of Diamonds
California — Death Valley
Colorado — Pikes Peak
Connecticut — Mystic Seaport
Delaware — Chesapeake and Delaware
    Canal
Florida — Everglades National Park
Georgia — Stone Mountain
Hawaii — Mauna Loa
Idaho — Hell's Canyon
Illinois — Sears Tower
Indiana — Indianapolis Motor Speedway
Iowa — Grotto of the Redemption
Kansas — Dodge City
Kentucky — Fort Knox
Louisiana — The French Quarter
Maine — Portland Head Light
Maryland — U.S. Naval Academy
Massachusetts — Plymouth Rock
Michigan — Automobile Factories
Minnesota — Source of Mississippi River
Mississippi — Vicksburg
Missouri — Mark Twain's Home
Montana — Little Bighorn Battlefield

Nebraska — Chimney Rock
Nevada — Hoover Dam
New Hampshire — Mount Washington
New Jersey — Atlantic City Boardwalk
New Mexico — Carlsbad Caverns
New York — Statue of Liberty
North Carolina — Great Smokey Mountain
    National Park
North Dakota — Geographic Center of
    North America
Ohio — Professional Football Hall of Fame
Oklahoma — Horse Show Capital of the
    World
Oregon — Crater Lake
Pennsylvania — Liberty Bell
Rhode Island — Narragansett Bay
South Carolina — Fort Sumter
South Dakota — Mount Rushmore
Tennessee — Grand Ole Opry
Texas — The Alamo
Utah — Great Salt Lake
Vermont — Green Mountain National Forest
Virginia — Williamsburg
Washington — Mount St. Helens
West Virginia — Harpers Ferry
Wisconsin — Wisconsin Dells
Wyoming — Yellowstone National Park

To Learn More . . .

Alabama — Tuskegee Institute

After opening in an old, abandoned church in 1881, the Tuskegee Institute grew, as the years passed, into a national model for schools desiring to teach vocational skills. Booker T. Washington founded the school to teach blacks to excel in carpentry, teaching, mechanics, and farming; and he remained 33 years at the Institute as principal and teacher. Another famous instructor, George Washington Carver, developed over 300 different products from the peanut plant.

Alaska — Mount McKinley

In the central part of Alaska rises the highest mountain in North America, Mount McKinley, also known as the "Top of the Continent." Named for 25th president William McKinley, the mountain is actually made up of two peaks: the north ascending to 19,470 feet and the south rising to 20,320 feet. In 1906 a climber made it to the top of the North Peak, and by 1913 a party of four men climbed the taller South Peak.

Arizona — Grand Canyon

Over a period of 6 million years, the Colorado River carved out the world's most spectacular canyon, the Grand Canyon, by cutting through layers of sandstone, limestone, shale, and granite to reveal different-colored layers which give viewers an ever-changing panorama of color throughout all daylight hours. Extending down 1 mile deep, the river uncovered rocks dating back 2 billion years! The Grand Canyon is not only 18 miles wide, but it stretches 220 miles long!

Arkansas — Crater of Diamonds

Near the town of Murfreesboro, in the southwestern part of Arkansas, lies the only major diamond field in the U.S. What is more, the public is invited to try their luck at searching the soil for their chance at fortune, too! Such things happen: the most valuable diamond unearthed was dubbed the "Uncle Sam" diamond, worth $250,000!

California — Death Valley

The lowest elevation in the entire Western Hemisphere lies along the eastern California border where the 130-mile long depression — named "Death Valley" by pioneers who had to cross it — lies surrounded by the Panamint, Grapevine, Black, and Funeral mountains. The desolate, desert environment is such that it is also the site of the hottest temperature ever recorded in America, when in 1913 the mercury reached 134° Fahrenheit!

Colorado — Pikes Peak

In 1805 Lieutenant Zebulon Pike was exploring the Upper Mississippi River, while fellow explorers Lewis and Clark were heading further west, when he attempted unsuccessfully to explore Minnesota in the wintertime. One would have thought he would have learned from that experience something about timing his journeys, but that was not to be the case after he left Minnesota. Proceeding southwest, he eventually sighted, from 150 miles away, the first of the Rocky Mountains that can be seen when approaching from the East. Pike unwisely started up this mountain in November, 1806, but only explored halfway up when he was forced back down due to lack of supplies. Nonetheless, the mountain bears his name and he attained fame in the slogan, "Pikes Peak or bust!" — a favorite saying of pioneers who headed west years later seeking land and gold.

Connecticut — Mystic Seaport

To return to the days of the tall ships of 100-200 years ago, one can visit the marvelously reconstructed seafront village of Mystic, Connecticut. There one can also see, moored at the docks, the *Charles W. Morgan*, New England's last wooden whaling ship, and also view one of the finest collections of clipper ship models in the U.S.

Delaware — Chesapeake & Delaware Canal

Crossing northern Delaware from Chesapeake Bay to Delaware Bay, this Canal shortens ship travel between Philadelphia and Baltimore by 285 miles. Additionally, it connects ports on the Chesapeake Bay with Wilmington, Delaware's chief port for foreign shipping.

Florida — Everglades National Park

Declared a National Park in 1947, the Everglades encompasses one of the largest swamp areas of the world, 2,746-square miles. The area had been uninhabited, even by any group of Indians, until 1842 when the Seminole Indians fled there after their wars with U.S. troops. It is home now to alligators, crocodiles, huge turtles, and manatees as well as over 300 different kinds of birds, which may be observed by walking the Arrhinga Trail, a boardwalk which extends far into this subtropical jungle.

Georgia — Stone Mountain

Just 16 miles west of Atlanta lies one of the largest domes of exposed granite in the world, rising 700 feet above the Georgia countryside. The idea of paying homage in stone to three Confederate leaders, Jefferson Davis, Robert E. Lee, and Thomas "Stonewall" Jackson resulted in a design upon which work was begun in 1923. Like Mount Rushmore, it was to be sculpted by Gutzon Borglum, but work on the mountain was discontinued in 1928. Fortunately work resumed in 1964, and by 1969 the landmark sculpture was finally completed.

Hawaii — Mauna Loa

One of the world's largest active volcanoes, Mauna Loa rises 13,677 feet above sea level, and to this day continues to spew lava from its sides. Although the volcanic activity occasionally increases, the last dangerous eruption, which buried a fishing village, was in 1950. The longest eruption of which there is a record lasted 18 months during 1855 and 1856.

Idaho — Hell's Canyon

Despite its forbidding name, the narrow Hell's Canyon gorge winds beautifully through Idaho on the Snake River about 100 miles south of Lewiston. As the river cuts through sheer rock walls at an average depth of 1 mile, at one point it reaches the actual deepest gorge in America — 7,900 feet below the cliff tops above.

Illinois — Sears Tower

The Sears Tower, in downtown Chicago, is the headquarters of the Sears Company, a famous clothing and home-furnishing retailer. Doubtless founder Richard Sears, who began the company by selling watches by mail in 1886, would be awed to gaze upon his building: 110 stories and 1,454 feet high — making it the tallest in the U.S.

Indiana — Indianapolis Motor Speedway

America's fascination with "getting there the fastest way possible" prompted the first 500-mile race at a track 6 miles northeast of downtown Indianapolis on May 30, 1911. Soon dubbed the "Indy 500," the annual race attracts spectators who watch drivers circle the 2.5-mile track at speeds near 200 miles per hour.

Iowa — Grotto of the Redemption

Just 2 weeks before his ordination in 1897, seminarian Paul Dobberstein grew seriously ill with pneumonia. He prayed for Our Blessed Mother's intercession and promised that if he were allowed to live, he would one day build her a shrine in thanksgiving. After a year's recuperation, he was assigned to the parish of Saints Peter and Paul in West Bend, Iowa, where he was to spend the remaining 57 years of his life. What began as one grotto of semi-precious stones and gems for Mary grew, over 42 years, into a series of nine grottos which tell the story of man's Fall from Grace, the lives of Our Redeemer and His Mother, and the Stations of the Cross.

Kansas — Dodge City

When, in 1872, the Santa Fe Railroad came through the site of Dodge City, no one knew it would become the stereotype of a "Wild West" town, the scene of cattle drives and gunfights. Located 100 miles east of Colorado, Dodge City was the largest cattle market in the world from 1875-1885 and saw the likes of lawmen Wyatt Earp and Bat Masterson enforce the law in what has been called the "Cowboy Capital of the World."

Kentucky — Fort Knox

One always first thinks of gold storage when thinking of Fort Knox, but it is also the U.S. Army Armored Headquarters containing the tank school, the armor board, and armor training center. Lying 35 miles south of Louisville, its public fame, of course, lies with the armored storage of $8 million in gold bullion. Furthermore, during World War II it was considered the safest place for storing copies of the U.S. Constitution, the Declaration of Independence, the Gettysburg Address, and the Magna Carta.

Louisiana — The French Quarter

An old New Orleans neighborhood named for the first settlers of the area, the French, the French Quarter might surprise the first-time visitor who had expected to find the architecture looking more French than Spanish. Although he would appreciate the beauty of the landscaped patios and the trademark lacy iron grillwork of fences and balconies, our visitor would still wonder at the Spanish influence. This stems from the fires of 1788 and 1794 which practically levelled the area. At the time of rebuilding, Spain controlled New Orleans, thus their architectural tastes prevailed.

Maine — Portland Head Light

One of the oldest and most famous of the lighthouses of our eastern seacoast, the Portland Head Light has proved essential to sailors and navigators since it was erected in 1791. Located near the city of South Portland, the lighthouse rises 101 feet above the rocks and pounding surf.

Maryland — U.S. Naval Academy

The U.S. Naval Academy has been training officers for the Navy and Marine Corps since its beginnings in 1845. Located on the western shore of Chesapeake Bay, this government-operated military college trains students, called "midshipmen," for 4 years so that they either enter the Navy as ensigns or enter the Marine Corps as second lieutenants.

Massachusetts — Plymouth Rock

None of the other 49 landmarks listed here has been "loved to pieces" as much as Plymouth Rock. Although popular legend has it that the Pilgrims actually stepped ashore *upon* this granite rock, it would have defied all navigational logic to steer toward this big boulder! Rather, the rock was nearby on that cold day, December 21, 1620. Nonetheless, as it did bear silent witness to the occasion, it was subsequently memorialized by being built into a wharf; moved and placed under an elm tree; and then moved again but dropped, broken, mended, and dragged, until it reached its current location in 1921 under its own granite canopy.

Michigan — Automobile Factories

Since more automobiles are produced in Detroit than anywhere else in the world, it is nicknamed "The Automobile Capital of the World" or "Motor City." In the early 1900s business executives Henry Ford, John and Horace Dodge, and Ransom Olds decided to take advantage of the large workforce and the choice location (at the hub of many good land and water routes) to ship in raw materials and ship out finished cars.

Minnesota — Source of the Mississippi River

The longest river in the U.S. starts as a small, clear stream flowing out of the north-western Minnesota's Lake Itasca to proceed 2,348 miles down to the Gulf of Mexico. Although one would have a hard time believing it as he stands in Cairo, Illinois, shading his eyes to see across the nearly 1-mile wide river, the Mississippi at its source is only 10 feet across and 2 feet deep, so visitors are able to step across it.

Mississippi — Vicksburg

Right in the middle of the Civil War, General Ulysses S. Grant began a bombardment of the city of Vicksburg, the last stronghold in the South controlling traffic on the Mississippi River. Since the Mississippi and its tributaries drain almost all the plains between the Appalachian and Rocky Mountains, it was key for supplying the Union armies in the days before highways, airlines, and an extensive railroad system. After 47 days of constant firing during which the local citizens had taken to the caves on the river bluffs and been reduced to eating mules, the city surrendered, giving the Union control of the Mississippi and the West and marking a turning point of the War.

Missouri — Mark Twain's home

At age 4, little Samuel Clemens moved to the town of Hannibal in 1839. Just as Samuel took on a new name, Mark Twain, to become an author, so also did his boyhood town Hannibal become immortalized as "St. Petersburg" in his most famous book, *Tom Sawyer*. We may assume Twain loved the town of his youth since St. Petersburg means "St. Peter's town" — that is, Heaven.

Montana — Little Bighorn Battlefield

In 1876 the U.S. Army was taking Sioux and Cheyenne Indians to reservations when General George Custer received orders from his commander to locate and confirm reports of an Indian village ahead. Upon finding it, Custer ordered an immediate attack, severely underestimating the number of warriors in the village. Custer had 650 men at his disposal, and he thought there were 1,000 Indians, including women and children, in the village. In reality, it was the largest gathering of hostile Indians in the history of the West, numbering close to 5,000 warriors. As there were no survivors from Custer's command, the battle has come to be known as "Custer's Last Stand."

Nebraska — Chimney Rock

At the end of a long trip, it is always a relief to gain sight of a familiar landmark to let you know you're almost home, or at least making some progress. Such was the feeling of pioneers heading west across the seemingly endless plains of Nebraska when, about 40 miles east of the Wyoming border, they sighted the 500-foot remains of a volcano. All that was and is left is the core of the volcano, time and erosion having worn away all else, leaving a vertical tower of igneous rock that looks like a lonesome chimney of a ruined house. Now the pioneers faced the prospect of crossing the Rockies!

Nevada — Hoover Dam

Built in the 1930s for flood control, Hoover Dam also took the waters of the Colorado River and, allowing them to fall through huge turbines, became a source of electric power to Arizona, California, and Nevada. One of the highest concrete dams in the world, the Dam features elevators which descend the equivalent of 44 stories into its interior, but still do not reach the base. Located only 25 miles southeast of Las Vegas, Hoover Dam is a common side trip for tourists to that city.

New Hampshire — Mount Washington

Mount Washington is the highest peak in the northeastern U.S., towering 6,288 feet in the Presidential Range of the White Mountains. It is the site of the fastest wind speed ever recorded in America — there the wind blew an incredible 231 m.p.h. in 1934!

New Jersey — Atlantic City Boardwalk

Along the southeastern coast of New Jersey is situated one of the largest seaside resorts in the world, Atlantic City. When in Atlantic City, a "must see" is the 7-mile long "Boardwalk," winding its way along the ocean and made famous in the family game Monopoly, as were other streets of the town. Lined with theaters, shops, hotels, and restaurants, the wooden sidewalk also fronts Convention Hall, the traditional site of the annual Miss America contest.

New Mexico — Carlsbad Caverns

In 1901 cowboy Jim White began to explore the mouth of a cave in southeastern New Mexico, little dreaming of the fantastic world of stalactites and stalagmites he would find inside. We may never know the extent of this chain of underground caves which are thought to have been formed from water hollowing out limestone 60 million years ago, the time of the formation of the Rocky Mountains. Incredibly beautiful formations and huge "rooms" as large

as 4 football fields delight visitors who can also witness the exodus of millions of bats at dusk from mid-March through October.

New York — Statue of Liberty

One of the largest and most famous statues in the world, the Statue of Liberty was a gift to the people of the U.S. from the people of France to celebrate freedom from tyranny and the prospects of a better life through freedom. In 1884 the French people donated $250,000 and the American people $280,000 for a pedestal to execute the design of Auguste Bartholdi. Builder of the Eiffel Tower, Alexandre Eiffel, supervised the actual building of the statue which features copper sheets over a skeleton of iron. Officially named "Liberty Enlightening the World," the statue graces Liberty Island in New York Harbor.

North Carolina — Great Smokey Mountain National Park

Along the border of Tennessee and North Carolina lie the Great Smokey Mountains, wrapped in the bluish haze that helped named them. The rugged mountains boast 53 peaks over 1 mile high; the tallest is Clingmans Dome at 6,643 feet. The National Park, established in 1930, also encompasses the most extensive virgin hardwood and red-spruce forests in America.

North Dakota — Geographic Center of North America

Approximately 2,000 miles from both the eastern and western borders of North America, as well as 2,250 miles from the northern and southern borders, lies the little town of Rugby, North Dakota, making it the geographic center of our continent. A cartographer, or map-maker, would plot it at about Lat. 48° N, Long. 100° W.

Ohio — Pro Football Hall of Fame

Dedicated in 1962, the Professional Football Hall of Fame in Canton, Ohio, honors players, coaches, and others who have made outstanding contributions to what has developed into America's most popular spectator sport.

Oklahoma — Horse Show Capital of the World

Every year the American Horse Shows Association approves over 1,500 shows, and Oklahoma hosts more than its share, as well as being home to the Cowboy Hall of Fame and the National Finals Rodeo. Horse shows are generally divided into 3 categories: performance, breeding, and equitation. In the first type of competition the horses are judged for abilities such as jumping and driving. Breeding shows feature horses of all the same breed whose physical qualities are compared so as to name one horse "best of breed." Finally, equitation shows are "horsemanship" shows in which riders are judged for their style and control of their horse.

Oregon — Crater Lake

The deepest lake in the U.S. was formed 6,600 years ago when Mt. Mazama, a volcano, in the Cascade Mountain Range, collapsed. This created a hollowed-out bowl which filled over the years with rain water, forming today's brilliantly blue waters of Crater Lake. Situated as it is, Crater Lake has no known outlets or inlets feeding it. As mentioned, it is America's deepest lake, plunging to 1,932 feet at its deepest and covering a 20-square-mile area.

Pennsylvania — Liberty Bell

Like the Statue of Liberty, another symbol of freedom in America, the Liberty Bell, hangs in Philadelphia, bearing an inscription from Leviticus 25:10, "Proclaim Liberty throughout all the land unto all inhabitants thereof." The Liberty Bell was cast in 1753 in London, unfortunately cracking soon after its arrival in America that same year. After it was fixed, it announced the adoption of the Declaration of Independence by ringing out on July 8, 1776; and was rung on that anniversary annually until it again cracked while tolling for the funeral of the first Chief Justice of the Supreme Court, John Marshall, in 1835. Thereafter, it would no longer be rung but has been "struck" on special occasions, such as the Normandy Invasion on D-Day in World War II.

Rhode Island — Narragansett Bay

A narrow arm of the Atlantic Ocean extending 28 miles into the state of Rhode Island, Narragansett Bay contains the actual island "Rhode Island" itself; and we find the capital, Providence, situated on the Bay's western shore. Twenty miles across at its widest, the Bay is the home of hundreds of harbors and resorts, including the famous town of Newport.

South Carolina — Fort Sumter

When South Carolina decided to leave the Union in April, 1861, it prepared to seize the U.S. forts in Charleston Harbor. Major Robert Anderson was in command of Fort Sumter when General Pierre Beauregard demanded Anderson's surrender.

After several days of bombardment, Beauregard gained his objective and allowed Anderson and his troops to leave unharmed with their weapons and flag. Thus the Civil War officially began.

South Dakota — Mount Rushmore

Sculptor Gutzon Borglum designed and supervised the metamorphosis of the granite Mount Rushmore into one of the most recognizable monuments in the world: a tribute to 4 American presidents, George Washington, Thomas Jefferson, Theodore Roosevelt, and Abraham Lincoln. After 14 years of drilling and dynamiting from 1927 to 1941, workers unveiled the colossal sculpture in which Washington's head is as tall as a 5-story building!

Tennessee — Grand Ole Opry

The traditional music of the rural South began to enjoy a much wider audience with the development of the recording and broadcasting industries in the 1920s. Radio programs sent, over the airwaves, the sounds of barn dances and country jamborees to the people of the South and Midwest. The most famous of these programs was the "Grand Ole Opry," which also referred to the place from which it was broadcast, the old opera house in Nashville. From 1925-1974 devoted listeners tuned in to hear established and up-and-coming stars play and sing. After 1974, the program moved to nearby Opryland.

Texas — The Alamo

In 1718 San Antonio de Valero was built as a Catholic mission in what became southwestern Texas, but which was then northern Mexico. Originally high walls encompassed a monastery and church, and the mission came to be known by the nickname "The Alamo," Spanish for "cottonwood," referring to the trees which grew nearby. By 1836 relations between American settlers and the Mexican government were so strained that the settlers determined to fight for their independence from Mexico. General Santa Anna, with 5,000 men, bombarded the Alamo from February 23 to March 6, the historic date when he ordered a predawn attack upon the 187 defenders of the Alamo. Although all 187 men were killed, this massacre inspired other Texans to "Remember the Alamo!" defeating Santa Anna within two months.

Utah — Great Salt Lake

Originally part of the huge freshwater Lake Bonneville, the Great Salt Lake continues to be fed by freshwater streams; but as there are no outlets, the waters never drain; rather, they dry up, leaving behind the salt they had picked up. Only small brine shrimp can call its waters home, but swimmers delight in bobbing around like corks in the excessively salty lake. Tons of common salt are taken from the Great Salt Lake each year.

Vermont — Green Mountain National Forest

As part of the Appalachian chain, the Green Mountains of Vermont are one of the oldest ranges in America; thus, water, wind, and ice have worn down the peaks. Originally the Green Mountains, *vert mont* in French, were named for the evergreens that covered them; nowadays visitors also enjoy maple, birch, ash, and hemlock trees, too. Running as they do, north and south along the central length of the state, the mountains serve as a sort of "backbone" of the state. They are also the site of historic battlegrounds and are part of the Appalachian Trial along the crests.

Virginia — Williamsburg

On the peninsula between the James and York Rivers lay Williamsburg, which was named to honor King William III of England and which served as the capital of the Virginia colony from 1699-1776 and later of the state (commonwealth) of Virginia from 1776-1780. When, in the early 20th century, people started to bemoan the rundown condition of this historic town, financier John D. Rockefeller funded an extensive renovation which restored over 80 original buildings to their 1700s appearance. Today visitors can stroll among these buildings, watching and listening to costumed craftsmen demonstrate such skills as barrelmaking, candledipping, cabinetmaking, and more.

Washington — Mount St. Helens

The mainland of the U.S. had not witnessed a volcanic eruption outside Alaska since 1921 when, in 1980, Mount St. Helens erupted. Located in the Cascade Mountains, less than 100 miles from Seattle, Mount St. Helens spewed forth lava and hot ash which started forest fires and also melted mountain snow covers. This led to flooding and mud slides, resulting in 60 deaths.

West Virginia — Harpers Ferry

Tensions over the slavery issue were reaching the breaking point when, in 1859, abolitionist John Brown captured the U.S. arsenal at Harpers Ferry (then in Virginia), about 55 miles northwest of Washington, D.C. on the Potomac River. Brown had planned to arm slaves, urging them to rebel, but he was unable to leave the arsenal under the heavy fire of U.S. troops led by Robert E. Lee. After 2 days, Brown was forced out, tried, and hanged. That western area of Virginia went on, itself, to "secede" from Virginia and remained with the Union as the state of West Virginia throughout the Civil War.

Wisconsin — The Wisconsin Dells

A boat trip along the Wisconsin River in south central Wisconsin will take visitors along a 7-mile stretch where the river has cut through soft sandstone to create beautiful rock formations which bear such interesting names as "Grand Piano," "Devil's Elbow," and "Fat Man's Misery."

Wyoming — Yellowstone National Park

The first area in the U.S. to be designated as national park seems a "shoe-in" considering its spectacular features. Created 60,000 years ago by volcanic action, Yellowstone National Park is world-famous for its hot springs, bubbling mud, and spouting geysers which continue to be fueled by the magma under the earth's surface. Landmark geyser Old Faithful, which spouts every 80 minutes, is only one of 200 geysers in the park. Furthermore, Yellowstone is home to America's largest wildlife preserve where bears, elk, bison, cougars, moose, and mule deer roam freely on the ground, while bald eagles, white pelicans, blue herons, and trumpeter swans claim the skies and waters.

State Catholic Fact

Alabama — Ave Maria Grotto replicas
Alaska — Christ the King Statue on King Island
Arizona — Mission San Xavier del Bac
Arkansas — Shrine of Our Lady of the Ozarks
California — Bl. Junipero Serra's missions
Colorado — Sacred Heart Shrine near Golden
Connecticut — Priests not permitted until 1818
Delaware — First mission before 1750
Florida — St. Augustine, first Catholic parish in U.S.
Georgia — Flannery O'Connor born in Savannah
Hawaii — Bl. Damien de Veuster's ministry to lepers
Idaho — Sacred Heart Mission, oldest building in Idaho
Illinois — St. Frances Cabrini died in Chicago
Indiana — Fr. Julius Nieuwland developed neoprene
Iowa — Luxembourgian settlers founded St. Donatus
Kansas — St. Philippine Duchesne worked with Potawatomi Indians
Kentucky — Bardstown, first Catholic settlement
Louisiana — St. John Berchmans's miracle for Mary Wilson
Maine — Site of first Mass offered in New England
Maryland — First English colony to permit the Mass
Massachusetts — Annual blessing of fishing fleet
Michigan — St. Isaac Jogues preached near Sault Ste. Marie
Minnesota — Fr. Hennepin named St. Anthony Falls (Minneapolis)
Mississippi — Site of first seminary to admit African-Americans
Missouri — St. Philippine Duchesne died in St. Charles
Montana — Fr. De Smet established first mission
Nebraska — Priestly Fraternity of St. Peter established seminary in 1998
Nevada — Former gold miner, Fr. Monogue, missionary
New Hampshire — NH constitution barred Catholic officeholders
New Jersey — Headquarters of the Blue Army of Fatima
New Mexico — Shrine of Our Lord of Esquipulas
New York — National Shrine of North American Martyrs
North Carolina — First Catholic church not built until 1823
North Dakota — Fr. Dumoulin was first Catholic missionary
Ohio — Shrine of the Holy Relics, largest collection in world
Oklahoma — Abbey of Fontgombault, France, established daughter house in 1999
Oregon — Fr. Blanchet celebrated the first Mass in 1838
Pennsylvania — Former Russian prince, Fr. Gallitzin, established Loretto
Rhode Island — First Catholic church not built until 1829
South Carolina — Missionary attempt as early as 1569
South Dakota — Fr. Ravoux published Dakota language prayer book
Tennessee — Replica of Shrine at Banneux, Belgium
Texas — Explorer LaSalle's priests martyred
Utah — First-known missionary priests arrived in 1776
Vermont — Ethan Allen's daughter, Frances, converted and became a nun
Virginia — Missionary attempt as early as 1526
Washington — First missionary priests arrived in 1838
West Virginia — First Catholic church founded in 1835
Wisconsin — Fr. Marquette erected cross at site of Holy Hill
Wyoming — Fr. De Smet celebrated first Mass in 1840

To Learn More . . .

Alabama — Ave Maria Grotto Replicas
Ave Maria Grotto, near Cullman, displays over 120 miniature replicas of famous churches and shrines.

Alaska — Christ the King Statue on King Island
On King Island, in the Bering Sea, stands a bronze statue of Christ the King, erected in 1937, by Rev. Bernard Hubbard, S.J.

Arizona — Mission San Xavier del Bac
The Mission San Xavier del Bac, near Tucson, is one of the most complete and beautiful missions surviving from the colonial period. It was founded in 1700 by Father Eusebio Kino.

Arkansas — Shrine of Our Lady of the Ozarks
The Shrine of Our Lady of the Ozarks stands near U.S. Highway 71, in the northwestern corner of Arkansas.

California — Blessed Junipero Serra's Missions
Blessed Junipero Serra established several missions in California in the 18th century, including San Carlos Borromeo in Carmel and San Juan Capistrano.

Colorado — Sacred Heart Shrine near Golden
St. Frances Cabrini established a shrine of the Sacred Heart near Golden.

Connecticut — Priests Not Permitted Until 1818
Despite the Bill of Rights, Catholic priestly ministry was not permitted in Connecticut until 1818.

Delaware — First Mission
The first mission in Delaware was established before 1750 in New Castle County.

Florida — St. Augustine: Oldest Parish
St. Augustine, the first Catholic parish in the present U.S., was established in 1565.

Georgia — Flannery O'Connor Birthplace
Catholic author of fiction Flannery O'Connor was born in Savannah and lived most of her life and died in Milledgeville, which is east of Macon.

Hawaii — Blessed Damien de Veuster's Ministry
Blessed Damien de Veuster ministered to the lepers on Molokai until he himself died from leprosy in 1889.

Idaho — Sacred Heart Mission Built
The oldest building in Idaho is the Sacred Heart Mission in Cataldo, built by the Couer d'Alene Indians in the 1850s.

Illinois — St. Frances Cabrini's Death
St. Frances Cabrini, founder of the Missionary Sisters of the Sacred Heart, expended much of her energy on missions in Chicago, and she died there at Columbus Hospital in 1917.

Indiana — Fr. Julius Nieuwland Developed Neoprene
Fr. Julius Nieuwland helped to develop the synthetic rubber neoprene at the University of Notre Dame during the 1920s and 30s.

Iowa — Settlers from Luxembourg Found St. Donatus
The town of St. Donatus, in eastern Iowa, was established by Catholic settlers from Luxembourg, who brought with them a devotion to Our Lady of Consolation.

Kansas — St. Philippine Duchesne's Work with Indians
St. Philippine Duchesne, foundress of the American branch of the Society of the Sacred Heart, worked among the Potawatomi Indians near Mound City in eastern Kansas.

Kentucky — Bardstown Founded
The first Catholic settlement in Kentucky was at Bardstown and was established in 1775.

Louisiana — St. John Berchmans's Miracle
In 1866, at the Academy of the Sacred Heart in Grand Coteau, Mary Wilson received an apparition of then-uncanonized John Berchmans and was cured of a serious illness. This miracle led to the canonization of Berchmans.

Maine — First Mass Offered in New England
The first Mass offered in New England took place in 1604 on Ste. Croix (now DeMont's) Island and was said by Rev. Nicholas Aubry.

Maryland — First English Colony to Permit Mass
Maryland was the first English colony in America which permitted Catholic worship under its charter of 1634.

Massachusetts — Annual Blessing of Fishing Fleet
Gloucester, Massachusetts, is the site of the annual blessing of the fishing fleet by the bishop.

Michigan — St. Isaac Jogues Preached
The first evangelization in Michigan took place near Sault Ste. Marie. The priests who preached

to the Chippewa were the Jesuits St. Isaac Jogues and Fr. Charles Rayonbaut.

Minnesota — Fr. Hennepin Named Waterfall
St. Anthony Falls, near the site of present-day Minneapolis, was named in 1630 by Fr. Louis Hennepin, who had been captured by the Dakota Indians along with two companions.

Mississippi — First Integrated Seminary
St. Augustine Seminary, in Bay St. Louis, was the first seminary in the U.S. to admit African-American candidates for the priesthood.

Missouri — St. Philippine's Death
St. Philippine Duchesne died in 1852 in St. Charles, Missouri, where she had gone to serve the Potawatomi Indians.

Montana — Fr. De Smet's Mission
The first mission to Montana was established in 1841 by Fr. Pierre Jean De Smet, the Belgian Jesuit.

Nebraska — FSSP Seminary at Denton
The Priestly Fraternity of St. Peter (FSSP) established a seminary in Denton in 1998.

Nevada — Former Gold Miner, Fr. Monogue
One of the earliest missionary priests to Nevada was Rev. Patrick Monogue, who, before his vocation, had mined for gold in California.

New Hampshire — Constitution Barred Catholic Officeholders
Because of anti-Catholic prejudice, the New Hampshire state constitution barred Catholics from public office until as late as 1877.

New Jersey — The Blue Army of Fatima
The national headquarters of the Blue Army of Fatima is located at the Shrine of the Immaculate Heart of Mary in Washington.

New Mexico — Shrine of Our Lord of Esquipulas
The Shrine of Our Lord of Esquipulas was built in 1816 in Chimayo, in northern New Mexico. It is known as the "Lourdes of America" due to the many healings that have occurred there.

New York — National Shrine of the North American Martyrs
Auriesville, New York, is the site of the martyrdom of the French Jesuits Br. Rene Goupil, Fr. Isaac Jogues, and Br. John Leangle in 1642 and 1646. The site is now home to the National Shrine of the North American Martyrs.

North Carolina — First Church Built in 1823
The first Catholic church in North Carolina, St.

John the Evangelist in Washington, was not built until 1823.

North Dakota — Fr. Dumoulin, Missionary
The first Catholic missionary in North Dakota was Fr. Joseph Severe Dumoulin, who was sent after 1818 to minister to French Canadian refugees from the Winnipeg area.

Ohio — Shrine of the Holy Relics
The Shrine of the Holy Relics in Maria Stein, Ohio, may contain the largest collection of relics in the world.

Oklahoma — Fontgombault Daughter House
In 1999 the French Benedictine monastery of Fontgombault established a daughter house at Clear Creek, east of Tulsa.

Oregon — First Mass Celebrated by Fr. Blanchet
The first Mass in Oregon took place at St. Paul in 1839 and was offered by Fr. Francoix Blanchet.

Pennsylvania — Former Russian Prince Established Loretto
Loretto, in central Pennsylvania, is the Catholic settlement established in 1799 by Demetrius Gallitzin, who was born a Russian prince, raised as an atheist, but was ordained a Catholic priest in 1795.

Rhode Island — First Catholic Church Built 1829
The first Catholic church in Rhode Island was built in Pawtucket in 1829.

South Carolina — Missionary Attempts in 1569
The first missionary attempt in South Carolina took place in 1569, when Fr. John Rogel established a chapel in Port Royal Sound.

South Dakota — Dakota Language Prayer Book
In 1843 Rev. Augustin Ravoux published a prayer book in the Dakota Indian language.

Tennessee — Shrine of Banneux Replica
A replica of the shrine at Banneux stands near New Hope.

Texas — La Salle's Priests Martyred
Priests accompanying the Sieur de La Salle were the first to establish missions in Texas, at Matagorda, in 1685, and were also the first martyrs in Texas: Fr. Zenobius Membre, Fr. Maximum Le Clercq, and Fr. Chefdeville.

Utah — Missionary Priests Arrived in 1776
The first priests to preach to the Indians in Utah were Frs. Silvestre de Escalante and Atanasio Dominquez, who were sent from Santa Fe in 1776.

Vermont — Frances Allen Converted

Frances Allen, the daughter of Ethan Allen, who led the famous Green Mountain Boys in the Revolutionary War, converted to Catholicism in 1808 and became a nun at Hotel-Dieu in Montreal.

Virginia — Missionary Attempt in 1526

Spanish missionaries preached to the Indians in Virginia almost a century before English settlement began. In 1526 and 1570 priests were sent to Virginia, but the hostility and violence of the natives led to the end of the missionary effort.

Washington — Missionary Priests Arrived in 1838

The first Catholic missionaries came to Washington from Canada in 1838 and settled in the area of Vancouver on the Columbia River.

West Virginia — First Catholic Church Founded in 1835

The first Catholic church in what would become West Virginia was founded about 1835 in Martinsburg.

Wisconsin — Fr. Marquette at Site of Holy Hill

Near Hubertus, northwest of Milwaukee, is the Shrine of Our Lady of Holy Hill, Wisconsin's oldest shrine. It is believed that Fr. Marquette erected a cross on this hill in the 1670s. Shrines and chapels have been added in 1858, 1881, 1938, and 1956.

Wyoming — Fr. De Smet Celebrated First Mass

Fr. Pierre-Jean De Smet, S.J., arrived in Wyoming in 1840 and probably said the first Mass in the Wyoming Territory.

Learn more about these Catholic Americans . . .

Alfred E. Smith
Archbishop John Lamy
Bishop Francis Blanchet
Bishop John Carroll
Bishop John Dubois
Bishop John England
Bishop Joseph Machebeuf
Bishop Simon Brute
Blessed Francis Xavier Seelos
Blessed Mother Theodore Guerin
Brother Joseph Dutton
Cardinal James Gibbons
Cardinal Terence Cooke
Charles Carroll of Carrollton
Colonel William Cody (Buffalo Bill)
Daniel Carroll
Dorothy Day
Doctor Tom Dooley
Elizabeth Clovis Lange
    (Mother Mary Elizabeth)
Father Anthony Blanc
Father Antonio Margil
Father Benedict Flaget
Father Edward Flanagan
Father Edward Sorin
Father Emil J. Kapaun

Father Eusebio Kino
Father Gabriel Richard
Father John David
Father Joseph Timothy O'Callahan, S.J.
Father Juan de Padilla
Father Louis Hennepin
Father Michael McGivney
Father Stephen Badin
Father Thomas Frederick Price
Father Vince Capodanno
Joyce Kilmer
Kit Carson
Mother Catherine Spalding
Mother Henriette Delille
Mother M. Xavier Warde
Mother Marianne Cope
Sister Blandina Segale
Saint Elizabeth Ann Seton
Saint John Neumann
Saint Katharine Drexel
Venerable Father Solanus Casey
Venerable Pierre Toussaint
Venerable Rose Hawthorne Lathrop
    (Mother Mary Alphonsa)

See page 105.

State Historical Fact

Alabama — Montgomery was site of the first Confederate capital
Alaska — U.S. bought Alaska for $7.2 million in 1867
Arizona — Oraibi, oldest continuously inhabited site, from 1100s
Arkansas — De Soto explored in 1541
California — Discovery of gold at Sutter's Mill
Colorado — Gold discovered at Cherry Creek in 1858
Connecticut — First nuclear submarine, *Nautilus*, built and launched at Groton
Delaware — First state to ratify U.S. Constitution
Florida — St. Augustine, oldest continuously settled town in U.S.
Georgia — Capture of Atlanta, turning point of Civil War
Hawaii — Japanese attacked Pearl Harbor
Idaho — World's first electricity generated from nuclear energy
Illinois — Chicago fire of 1871
Indiana — Battle of Tippecanoe led by William Henry Harrison in 1811
Iowa — First U.S. center for study of child development
Kansas — Quantrill's raid on Lawrence in Civil War
Kentucky — Daniel Boone arrived in 1769
Louisiana — Battle of New Orleans led by Andrew Jackson
Maine — Doughnut hole invented by Capt. Gregory in 1847
Maryland — Francis Scott Key wrote the "Star-Spangled Banner"
Massachusetts — Revolutionary War began
Michigan — Henry Ford's first automobile factory
Minnesota — Schoolcraft discovered source of Mississippi River
Mississippi — Vicksburg was captured after a 47-day siege in 1863
Missouri — Oregon and Santa Fe Trails began in Independence
Montana — Custer's Last Stand at Battle of Little Bighorn in 1876
Nebraska — First Arbor Day celebrated in 1872
Nevada — Kit Carson guided Frémont expedition from 1843 to 1845
New Hampshire — Nation's oldest tax-supported free library
New Jersey — Victory at Trenton for George Washington
New Mexico — Oldest road in U.S.: Santa Fe to Chihuahua
New York — Nation's first capital was New York City
North Carolina — First airplane flight at Kitty Hawk
North Dakota — First explorer, de la Verendrye, arrived 1738
Ohio — Commodore Perry secured Lake Erie during War of 1812
Oklahoma — Biggest land run, 50,000 settlers on first day, occurs on 9/16/1893
Oregon — Lewis and Clark's westernmost explorations
Pennsylvania — Declaration of Independence signed
Rhode Island — First gas lamps in U.S. introduced in Newport in 1806
South Carolina — Civil War began at Fort Sumter
South Dakota — "Wild Bill" Hickok shot to death in Deadwood
Tennessee — Battle of Shiloh in 1862 resulted in 23,000 deaths
Texas — 1900 hurricane killed 6,000 people
Utah — Transcontinental Railroad met at Promontory in 1869
Vermont — Northernmost land action of Civil War at St. Albans
Virginia — Surrender at Appomattox ended Civil War
Washington — Grand Coulee Dam, largest work of masonry ever, completed in 1942
West Virginia — John Brown's raid on Harpers Ferry in 1859
Wisconsin — First typewriter designed in Milwaukee in 1867
Wyoming — Yellowstone became first U.S. National Park

To Learn More . . .

Alabama — Montgomery was First Confederate Capital
From February 8 to May 21, 1861, the first Confederate capital was Montgomery, thus earning it the title, "Cradle of the Confederacy." Confederate President Jefferson Davis was inaugurated there. When Virginia joined the Confederacy, the Confederate Congress voted to move the capital to Richmond since Virginia was the most important state in the Confederacy, both economically and politically.

Alaska — Bought for $7.2 million in 1867
In 1867 U.S. Secretary of State William H. Seward paid Russia $7.2 million, or about two cents per acre, for the territory which would become the state of Alaska. Russia wanted to sell it to meet the mounting expenses of the Crimean War. But the decision was not immediately popular with the American public who could not see the worth of what seemed to be a frozen wasteland, calling the territory "Seward's Folly" and "Seward's Icebox."

Arizona — Oraibi is Oldest Continuously Inhabited Site
Probably the oldest continuously inhabited settlement in the U.S., Oraibi was built by Hopi Indians during the 1100s. In northeastern Arizona, it is one of 11 villages on or near 3 high mesas of the present-day Hopi reservation. Like their early ancestors, many Hopi raise small herds of sheep and grow crops on plots of valley land. Some Hopi earn additional money selling kachina dolls, which represent messengers sent by their gods. At certain times of the year, Hopi men dress as kachinas and perform dances in the village square or in underground structures called kivas.

Arkansas — De Soto Explored in 1541
In 1537 King Charles I of Spain appointed Hernando De Soto governor of Cuba. The king also gave De Soto the right to explore and conquer a region of North America that included many present-day southern states in our country. De Soto hoped to find gold there. The first European explorer to reach the Mississippi River, De Soto crossed it to continue his explorations to the west and south. Thus he was the first white man to visit what would become Arkansas. De Soto probably visited the Hot Springs area in 1541 before returning to the Mississippi. After regaining the river, he contracted a fever which proved fatal. De Soto's men weighted his body and buried it in the Mississippi. Almost 400 years later, in 1921, Congress made Hot Springs part of a national park.

California — Gold Discovered at Sutter's Mill
In 1839 John A. Sutter, a pioneer trader, was living on land that had been granted to him in the Sacramento Valley when he hired James W. Marshall, a carpenter, to help build a sawmill on the American River. There in 1849, at Sutter's Mill, Marshall found the first nuggets of gold. Of course, news of the gold discovery spread quickly, and thousands of people rushed to establish gold claims. These "forty-niners" poured into California from all parts of the world. Between 1848 and 1860, California's population increased from about 26,000 to 379,994.

Colorado — Gold Discovered at Cherry Creek in 1858
Colorado, then part of the New Mexico Territory, had few white settlers until prospectors discovered a major gold lode in 1858 at Cherry Creek, near the site of present-day Denver. This discovery led to a major boom of settlement, the motto of the immigrants being "Pikes Peak or Bust." By 1859 about 100,00 settlers had made their way to the gold fields. This population influx led Congress to establish the Colorado Territory in 1861.

Connecticut — First Nuclear Submarine Built at Groton
The *Nautilus*, the first nuclear submarine, was built at Groton, a Connecticut shipyard which had once produced whalers and clipper ships. In 1954, the Navy launched the *Nautilus* and on her first voyage, she broke all previous submarine records for underwater speed and endurance. In 1958, the *Nautilus* became the first submarine to sail under the ice at the North Pole.

Delaware — First State to Ratify the U.S. Constitution
Political leaders from Delaware and other colonies were dissatisfied with the Articles of Confederation, which were the predecessor of the Constitution. They urged the adoption of a stronger document. John Dickinson of Delaware helped James Madison of Virginia draft a new body of governing rules for the U.S. On December 7, 1787, Delaware voted unanimously to ratify, or approve, the U.S. Constitution. Delaware won the title of "The First State" since it was the first of the 13 original states to do so.

Florida — Oldest Continuously Settled Town — St. Augustine
Although "Fountain of Youth" explorer Ponce de Leon had visited the Atlantic coast of northeastern Florida in 1513, it was not until 1565 that a lasting settlement was developed there. Founded by Pedro Menendez de Aviles, a Spanish explorer, St. Augustine, as the village was known, has had residents ever since and thus rightly claims to be the "Oldest Continuously Settled Town" in America.

Georgia — Capture of Atlanta Seen as Turning Point of Civil War
As the Civil War dragged on, General William Tecumseh Sherman's army of 90,000 advanced on Atlanta, closing in on General Joseph E. Johnston, whose forces numbered 60,000. Johnston did not intend to fight Sherman unless his chances for victory were good. The Confederacy hoped to stall for time through the summer and fall of 1864, hoping that if they could hold out until the November elections, the war-weary Northern voters might remove Lincoln from office. When Sherman reached the outskirts of Atlanta, Jefferson Davis replaced Johnston with General John B. Hood, a more aggressive fighter. Hood's attacks, however, failed; Sherman was able to cut off Hood's supply lines; and on September 1, the Southern forces evacuated Atlanta. Sherman's men burned the town on their march to the sea, and the Atlanta campaign helped Lincoln win reelection.

Hawaii — Japanese Attack Pearl Harbor Drew U.S. into World War II
Pearl Harbor is one of the world's largest and best-sheltered harbors. Named for the pearl oysters that once grew there, it occupies about 10-square miles of navigable water and has 3 nearly landlocked lakes. Pearl Harbor was attacked by Japanese planes on December 7, 1941, forcing the U.S. into World War II. A 33-ship Japanese striking force that steamed under the cover of darkness to within 200 miles north of Oahu launched about 360 airplanes against the Pacific fleet. Eight American battleships were the primary targets of the first bombs which fell about 7:55 a.m. In all the U.S. had 18 ships sunk or severely damaged, 170 planes destroyed, and 3,700 casualties.

Idaho — Electricity Generated From Nuclear Energy for First Time
American and British scientists were able to harness the power of atomic energy to generate electricity. A nuclear reactor built at the National Reactor Testing Station near Idaho Falls powered a generator that produced the first electricity from atomic energy in 1951.

Illinois — Chicago Burns in Fire of 1871
The summer of 1871 was unusually dry in Chicago. Because only about a fourth the normal amount of rain fell between July and October, the city of Chicago, with all its wooden buildings, was practically a bonfire waiting to happen. Then, on the evening of October 8, 1871, a fire started on the southwest side of the city. While it is generally accepted that the fire started in Mrs. Patrick O'Leary's barn, it is perhaps only legend that it was caused by a cow kicking over a lighted lantern, setting straw ablaze. To make matters worse, there was a strong wind that night. Flames raced north and east through the city, leaping across the river and chasing panic-stricken families. Hundreds fled into the chilly waters of Lake Michigan. When the flames were finally put out 24 hours later, the totality of the destruction was evident. It wiped out the downtown area and most houses on the north side, killing at least 300, leaving 90,000 homeless, and destroying about $200 million worth of property.

Indiana — Future President Led Battle of Tippecanoe
In 1809 Indiana territorial governor William Henry Harrison negotiated a treaty with Indian leaders to gain land along the White and Wabash Rivers. Many Indians denounced the treaty, uniting under the Shawnee chief Tecumseh. Tecumseh's brother agitated for action on the Indians' part, so Harrison

organized the citizen militia and marched to the Indians' village on the Wabash and Tippecanoe Rivers. In the predawn of November 7, 1811, the brother, known as "The Prophet," attacked Harrison's forces. After several hours of hand-to-hand fighting, the Indians fled what became known as the Battle of Tippecanoe. Harrison campaigned for the presidency on the strength of this victory in 1840.

Iowa — First U.S. Center for Study of Child Development
Iowa established the nation's first center to study child development at Iowa City in 1917. Not only were the researchers interested in the physical process of "growing up," but also in changes in behavior, thought processes, emotions, and attitudes of the children. In all societies, children learn to communicate, to get along with other people, and to act intelligently and responsibly. Since our society also values literacy, or the ability to read and write, the researchers were also interested in this aspect of child development.

Kansas — William Quantrill Led Destructive Raid on Lawrence
After trying his hand at farming, gambling, and schoolteaching, William Quantrill left Kansas after being accused of stealing and murder. While on the run from the law, he formed a gang that terrorized Kansas and Missouri settlers who opposed slavery. On August 21, 1863, Quantrill and his men burned most of the town of Lawrence and killed about 150 people. Frank James, Jesse James's brother, rode with Quantrill's gang off and on and was with them the day of the Lawrence raid. When in 1865 the gang led a raid into Kentucky, Quantrill was killed.

Kentucky — Daniel Boone Arrived in 1769
Daniel Boone, accompanied by his brother Stuart and brother-in-law Stuart, followed an Indian trail called the "Warriors' Path" through the Cumberland Gap of the Appalachians, at the extreme southwestern tip of Virginia, into Kentucky. They had been living in the Yadkin Valley in North Carolina. The party found Kentucky completely unsettled, and they were pleased with the rich soil and vast herds of buffalo they saw. Although the group returned to North Carolina, in 1775 they set out to settle in Kentucky.

Louisiana — Future President Led Battle of New Orleans
The Battle of New Orleans was the last engagement of the War of 1812, fought on January 8, 1815. A treaty of peace had been signed 15 days before the battle took place, but it was not approved by the U.S. until a month later. Meanwhile, the British had sent an army of over 8,000 men to capture New Orleans. There were several possible routes to the city; but, fortunately for the Americans, the British chose to march straight toward the trenches prepared by General Andrew Jackson's troops. American artillery and infantry mowed down about 1,500 British soldiers, including their commanding officer, General Sir Edward Pakenham. There were few American casualties.

Maine — Doughnut Hole Invented
Invention of the doughnut hole in 1847 by Captain Hanson Gregory is still commemorated at Camden. Legend has it that Captain Gregory jammed his fried cake onto one of the spokes of his ship's wheel during a sudden storm. However, an article in *The Boston Post* in 1847 reported that Captain Gregory cut the hole with the lid of his ship's tin pepper box. It is unclear whether he cut the hole in the raw dough, yet to be fried, or in an already-fried cake.

Maryland — Star Spangled Banner Composed by Key
During the War of 1812, Francis Scott Key, an American lawyer, was sent aboard a truce ship in the harbor near Baltimore to negotiate the release of a prisoner, but fighting broke out during the negotiations. He overheard the British plan of attack so he was not allowed to leave the ship. After witnessing from the ship the bombardment of Fort McHenry on September 13-14, 1814, Key wrote the anthem as he was rowed ashore. He finished the final draft that night at an inn. Sung to the tune "To Anacreon in Heaven," it became immediately popular among Americans.

Massachusetts — Revolutionary War Begun
On April 18, 1775, Lieutenant General Thomas Gage set out with his British troops to destroy the colonists' military supply depot at Concord. Dr. Joseph Warren, having discovered the British plans,

sent Paul Revere and William Dawes to warn the Minuteman at Lexington, which is on the road to Concord. When the British forces arrived in Lexington on the morning of April 19, they were met by Minutemen under the command of Captain John Parker. It is uncertain which side fired the first shot, but the skirmish marked the beginning of the Revolutionary War.

Michigan — Henry Ford Revolutionized Automobile Industry
At the end of the 19th century, many individuals in various countries were experimenting with the development of automobiles. Henry Ford built his first automobile in 1896 and established the Ford Motor Company in 1903. Like the other automobile manufacturers, he initially produced cars only for wealthy customers; but he became the first manufacturer to realize that an automobile could be produced at a price that the less wealthy could afford. He began to produce this vehicle, the Model T, in 1908; it was the bestselling automobile for the next 20 years.

Minnesota — Henry Schoolcraft Discovered Source of Mississippi River
In the early 1800s it was believed that Zebulon Pike had discovered the source of the Mississippi River at what is now known as Cass Lake. Almost 30 years later, Henry Schoolcraft, doubting that Cass Lake was the true source, undertook an expedition to confirm his theory. Guided by Chippewa Indians and using small Indian canoes, Schoolcraft's party was able to travel up the stream which fed into Cass Lake. The stream, however, became too shallow for the canoes and they had to portage 6 miles to a lake which the Indians called Elk Lake. Schoolcraft wanted the lake to be named something that meant "true head," so he asked a missionary what the Latin words for this would be. The missionary told him that the Latin word for truth was *veritas,* and for head *caput*. Schoolcraft took the end of the first word and the beginning of the second to make the word "Itasca."

Mississippi — Vicksburg Captured After 47-day Siege
Right in the middle of the Civil War, General Ulysses S. Grant began a bombardment of the city of Vicksburg, the last stronghold in the South controlling traffic on the Mississippi River. Since the Mississippi and its tributaries drain almost all the plains between the Appalachian and Rocky Mountains, it was key for supplying the Union armies in the days before highways, airlines, and an extensive railroad system. After 47 days of constant firing during which the local citizens had taken to the caves on the river bluffs and been reduced to eating mules, the city surrendered, giving the Union control of the Mississippi and the West and marking a turning point of the War.

Missouri — Beginning of Santa Fe and Oregon Trails
Independence, where the Oregon and Santa Fe Trails began, became the "Gateway to the West" for pioneers in the mid-1800s. The 780-mile long Santa Fe Trail was first used by William Becknell in 1821. From the years 1822 and 1843, an average of about 80 wagons used the trail each year. But during the 1850s and 1860s travel increased greatly — more than 5,000 wagons crossed each year. The much longer Oregon Trail was first developed by fur traders and explorers. Benjamin Bonneville is given credit for leading the first wagons along it in the 1830s. Both trails were severe tests of travelers' strength and endurance: Indian attacks, disease, and scarce food and water were to be expected, if not downright common.

Montana — Little Bighorn Site of Custer's Last Stand
In 1876, the U.S. Army was taking Sioux and Cheyenne Indians to reservations when General George Custer received orders from his commander to locate and confirm reports of an Indian village ahead. Upon finding it, Custer ordered an immediate attack, severely underestimating the number of warriors in the village. Custer had 650 men at his disposal, and he thought there were 1,000 Indians, including women and children, in the village. In reality, it was the largest gathering of hostile Indians in the history of the West, numbering close to 5,000 warriors. As there were no survivors from Custer's command, the battle has come to be known as "Custer's Last Stand."

Nebraska — Nation's First Arbor Day
The first Arbor Day was celebrated in Nebraska on April 10, 1872. J. Sterling Morton, a newspaper publisher of Nebraska City, suggested the idea as a good way to enrich the soil and conserve moisture in this state of vast prairies. Prizes were offered for the groups and individuals planting the

most trees, and Nebraskans rose to the task, planting 1 million trees that first day. Upon Morton's death, the Nebraska state legislature changed the celebration of Arbor Day to April 22, Morton's birthday. Other states have adopted the custom, choosing different days depending on when it is most advantageous to plant in their climates.

Nevada — Kit Carson Guides Frémont Expedition from 1843 to 1845
Christopher (Kit) Carson (1809-1868), after growing up in Kentucky and Missouri, ran away to the New Mexico Territory, where he became a trapper, hunter, and guide. When the U.S. government commissioned John C. Frémont to explore and map some of its western territories in 1842, he in turn hired Carson to guide him. In 1843 Kit Carson led the first U.S. expedition into the area that would later became the state of Nevada. Kit Carson, a Catholic convert, went on to become one of the most famous frontiersmen of the Old West.

New Hampshire — Nation's Oldest Tax-Supported Free Library
The first efforts to make books available to everyone resulted in libraries that charged dues, which were then used to buy more books. Called subscription libraries, these owed their early success to Benjamin Franklin, who founded the first one in Philadelphia in 1731. But ideally, the people wanted libraries available to those unable to afford dues. The library in Peterborough, New Hampshire, founded in 1833, may be the nation's oldest tax-supported free library. This idea really caught on, necessitating a census of the country's libraries by the late 1840s.

New Jersey — George Washington Secured Victory at Trenton
After the loss of the important Fort Washington in Manhattan during the Revolutionary War, George Washington and his troops regrouped, while the British poured into New Jersey. British Major General William Howe decided not to go after Washington but instead enjoy the comfort of winter quarters. The British assigned Hessian, or German, soldiers to guard Trenton. Crossing the Delaware River on Christmas Night, 1776, one column of Washington's forces completely surprised the Hessians and took 1,000 prisoners. Reassured by this change of events, Washington's army won a stunning victory at Princeton just one week later.

New Mexico — Nation's Oldest Road — Santa Fe to Chihuahua
El Camino Real, the oldest road in the U.S., runs from Santa Fe to Chihuahua, Mexico. Reflecting the area's very long ties to Spanish culture, the name *"El Camino Real"* means "the royal road" in Spanish. First serving travelers on horseback in 1581, it now accommodates fast-moving automobiles and trucks along Interstate Highway 25.

New York — New York City was Nation's First Capital
George Washington took the oath of office as the nation's first president in New York City on April 30, 1789. New York City served as the first capital of the U.S. from 1785 to 1790. Then Philadelphia became the second site, acting as the capital from 1790 to 1800. Washington selected the current site of our nation's capital in 1791 and employed a French engineer, Pierre L'Enfant, to develop plans for the city of Washington, D.C., thus making it one of the few cities of the world to be designed before it was built. But George Washington died in 1799, just a year before Washington, D.C., became the capital.

North Carolina — First Airplane Flight at Kitty Hawk
Even as children, brothers Orville and Wilbur Wright were interested in mechanical things, earning money selling little mechanical toys they put together themselves. It was in their bicycle manufacturing shop, above their newspaper shop, that they read of the death of pioneer flier Otto Lilienthal in 1896; and they determined to read everything they could get their hands on about principles of flight. Finally, on December 17, 1903, after much experimentation, Orville, having won a coin toss, piloted the world's first power-driven, heavier-than-air machine at Kitty Hawk. But to Wilbur went the honor of making the longest flight that day, 59 seconds. Only 4 newspapers mentioned the story the next day.

North Dakota — de la Verendrye Explored in 1738
The first explorer of the North Dakota region reached a Mandan Indian village near the present-day

capital of Bismarck in 1738. He was Pierre Gaultier de Varennes, Sieur de la Verendrye, who was looking for a route west to the Pacific Ocean. The Mandan were one of 4 tribes which farmed central North Dakota peacefully.

Ohio — Commodore Perry Secured Lake Erie in War of 1812

Control of Lake Erie was won for the U.S. by Commodore Oliver Hazard Perry's victory over the British near Put-in-Bay in 1813. He had sailed on September 10, 1813, with 9 small ships to fight the British, but he suffered an initial setback when the largest of his ships, the *Lawrence,* was disabled. Perry rowed to another of his ships, the *Niagara,* and from it directed the successful bombardment of the 6 British ships, securing a surrender after just 15 minutes. In reporting the battle to the military commander of the West, General William Henry Harrison, Perry wrote his famous quote, "We have met the enemy and they are ours."

Oklahoma — Huge Land Run — 50,000 Claims in One Day

Responding to pressure from white settlers, the government opened central Oklahoma for settlement in April 22, 1889. About 50,000 people moved into Oklahoma by that evening, although not all staked claims that day. The cities of Guthrie and Oklahoma City gained populations of 10,000 each in a single day. Some people had literally "jumped the gun," sneaking into the new land before a pistol shot signalled the real opening. The people who arrived too soon, "Sooners," ran their horses hard on the actual first day and showed the tired horses to the honest settlers to "prove" they had just arrived! The greatest Oklahoma land run occurred at the opening of the Cherokee Outlet on September 16, 1893. More than 50,000 persons staked claims the first day in the 6.5-million-acre area.

Oregon — Lewis and Clark's Westernmost Explorations

After more than 2 years exploring the United States' newly acquired Louisiana Purchase, Meriwether Lewis and William Clark reached the Columbia River and pushed forward as quickly as possible in an effort to winter at the Pacific coast. Arriving in November, 1805, the party built Fort Clatsop, which sheltered members of the expedition during the winter of 1805-1806 at the mouth of the Columbia. Returning to Missouri, they had traveled almost 7,700 miles, learning a vast deal about the Indian tribes and natural resources of this region.

Pennsylvania — Declaration of Independence Signed

For over 10 years, bad feelings had been building between Great Britain and her colonies in America. The colonists requested a greater share in making decisions in matters that would affect them, but as time passed, the opposite happened as Britain mandated additional taxes and punitive measures for the colonies. At last it was decided the only course was to announce to the world that the colonies were free from Great Britain's control and to state the reasons why. Thomas Jefferson was selected by committee to write a rough draft. Although in the declaration Jefferson blamed Great Britain for many wrongdoings, he stated that all people have certain rights as creatures of God, as in the famous phrase, ". . . that among these are Life, Liberty and the pursuit of Happiness." The Declaration of Independence, proclaiming the freedom of the 13 colonies, was adopted at Independence Hall in Philadelphia on July 4, 1776, read to a large crowd on July 8, and signed by most members of the Continental Congress on August 2. Ever since, its magnificent language has been a model for countries the world over.

Rhode Island — Gas Lamps Introduced in Newport

A Scottish inventor, William Murdock, developed the first lamps which needed no wick but gave light by means of a small gas flame. In 1792 he amazed his friends by lighting his home with gas lamps, and by the early 1800s had seen his lamps dot the streets of London, making nighttime travel brighter and thus safer. The lamps, using gas made from coal, were introduced in the U.S. in 1806 by David Melville of Newport.

South Carolina — Civil War Began at Fort Sumter

When South Carolina decided to leave the Union in April 1861, it next prepared to seize the U.S.

forts in Charleston Harbor. Major Robert Anderson was in command of Fort Sumter when General Pierre Beauregard demanded Anderson's surrender. After several days of bombardment, Beauregard gained his objective and allowed Anderson and his troops to leave unharmed with their weapons and flag. Thus the Civil War officially began.

South Dakota — Wild Bill Hickok Fatally Wounded in Deadwood Saloon
James Butler "Wild Bill" Hickok won fame in the West as a marksman and lawman who enforced the law single-handedly. After stints as stagecoach driver, scout, and marshal of several towns, Wild Bill toured eastern states with Buffalo Bill's show. The year 1876 found him in the gold "boom" town of Deadwood, which had grown quickly after that year's gold strike. Hickok was shot fatally there while playing cards in a saloon.

Tennessee — Battle of Shiloh Claimed 23,000 Casualties
The Battle of Shiloh in 1862 ended in a victory for the North when Confederate troops tried to stop a Union advance on Cornith, Mississippi. The Southern generals had decided to attack Grant when each side's forces were about evenly matched — Union 42,000 and Confederacy 40,000 — and before reinforcements would arrive for Grant. The South almost accomplished a crushing defeat on the first day of the battle, named for a church which was on the battlefield. But Grant did get his reinforcements, 20,000 men, by the second day, and they forced a Southern retreat after 2 days of the bloodiest fighting of the entire Civil War. The Confederates lost over 10,000 men, including General Albert Sidney Johnston. The Union lost more than 13,000 men.

Texas — Galveston Hurricane Killed 6,000
Lacking modern weather forecasting instruments and tracking devices, the people of Galveston had virtually no warning of a tremendous hurricane which hit the island on September 8, 1900. Four days earlier, the Weather Bureau in Washington, D.C., had advised Galveston of a "Tropical disturbance moving northward over Cuba" heading for Florida. But as late as the morning of the 8th, Galvestonians anticipated just another "overflow," where the Gulf of Mexico might rise enough to flood streets. What they got was the worst natural disaster ever to hit North America: an exceedingly powerful storm which killed over 6,000 people. In response, the city then built a seawall 17 feet high which, when put to the test in 1911, forestalled a 14-foot hurricane storm tide — and this time only 12 lives were lost.

Utah — U.S. Linked by Transcontinental Railroad
Although the eastern U.S. was crisscrossed by railroads by 1860, none extended into the "Wild West." Finally, in 1863 the Central Pacific Railroad began to lay track heading west from a point near Omaha, Nebraska, and the Union Pacific Railroad began similarly, heading east from Sacramento, California. Both had to cross towering, rugged mountain ranges and transport supplies across long distances. By 1868 the work developed into a race between the two railroads to see which would lay the most track in the shortest time. The 2 tracks met on May 10, 1869, in the Promontory Mountains of northern Utah. That day North America became the first continent in the world to be traversed by a railroad that ran coast to coast.

Vermont — Northernmost Action of Civil War
In what turned out to be a rather slapstick affair, about 20 Confederate soldiers robbed banks in St. Albans in far northern Vermont in 1864 and then fled into Canada. Lieutenant Bennett Young of Kentucky had planned that by plundering the town to enrich the collapsing Confederate treasury and draw Union troops away from the fronts to protect the United States/Canada border, a war might be stirred up between Canada and the U.S. in the general uproar over the incident. The robbers did make off with $208,000 but had left behind, within easy reach, over twice that amount. Plans to burn down the town of St. Albans failed humorously, and even the townspeople who formed a posse to pursue the robbers contributed to mishaps. The robbers were rounded up, tried, and eventually released in Montreal; and it is doubtful much of the money ever reached the Confederate treasury.

Virginia — Appomattox Surrender Ended Civil War
When, in April 1865, General Grant had forced General Lee to evacuate Richmond and had also prevented Lee from joining reinforcements in North Carolina, Lee wrote Grant asking to arrange

surrender terms. In one of the supreme ironies of history, the 2 generals meet in a house belonging to a Wilmer McLean, in whose former home General Beauregard had had his headquarters during the very first action of the War, First Bull Run. Mr. McLean rightly stated that the war began and ended in his front parlor. The house being in the little country settlement of Appomattox Court House, it is recorded that there, on Sunday, April 9, 1865, the war, which cost more American lives than any other, ended.

Washington — Grand Coulee Dam Completed

Grand Coulee Dam, completed in 1942, is the largest piece of masonry ever built. Furthermore, it is the greatest single source of water power in our country. Situated about 90 miles northwest of Spokane, the dam is nearly 1 mile long (5,223 feet), and 550 feet high — or about the equivalent of a 46-story building. It has 3 power plants and consists of about 12 million cubic yards of concrete.

West Virginia — Harpers Ferry Raided by John Brown

Tensions over the slavery issue were reaching the breaking point when, in 1859, abolitionist John Brown captured the U.S. arsenal at Harpers Ferry (then in Virginia), about 55 miles northwest of Washington, D.C., on the Potomac River. Brown had planned to arm slaves, urging them to rebel, but he was unable to leave the arsenal under the heavy fire of U.S. troops led by Robert E. Lee. After 2 days, Brown was forced out, tried, and hanged. That western area of Virginia went on, itself, to "secede" from Virginia and remained with the Union, as the state of West Virginia, throughout the Civil War.

Wisconsin — First Practical Typewriter Designed in Milwaukee

Ever since the mid-1700s, inventors on both sides of the Atlantic had tried to come up with a typewriting machine that was fast, easy to use, accurate, and inexpensive. The first practical typewriter was designed by Milwaukee inventors Carlos Glidden, Christopher Latham Sholes, and Samuel W. Soulé in 1867. This model resembled a little piano. But Sholes continued to refine the design and in 1873 issued a model that looked very much like portable typewriters looked all the way through the 1980s and the coming of personal computers.

Wyoming — Yellowstone Named First National Park

The first area in the U.S. to be designated as a national park seems a "shoe-in" considering its spectacular features. Created 60,000 years ago by volcanic action, Yellowstone National Park is world-famous for its hot springs, bubbling mud, and spouting geysers which continue to be fueled by the magma under the earth's surface. Landmark geyser Old Faithful, which spouts every 80 minutes, is only one of 200 geysers in the park. Furthermore, Yellowstone is home to America's largest wildlife preserve where bears, elk, bison, cougars, moose, and mule deer roam freely on the ground, while bald eagles, white pelicans, blue herons, and trumpeter swans claim the skies and waters.

Super Challenge for the Super Student

What did the Bishops of the United States proclaim at the First Council of Baltimore in 1846?

See page 103.

State Name Derivation

Alabama — Alibamu Indian, "plant gatherer"
Alaska — Aleutian Indian, "mainland"
Arizona — Papago Indian, "small spring"
Arkansas — Quapaw Indian, "downstream people"
California — In reference to a treasure island in a Spanish story
Colorado — Spanish, "red"
Connecticut — Algonquin Indian, "beside long, tidal river"
Delaware — Lord De La Warr
Florida — Spanish, "Easter" (*Pascua Florida*)
Georgia — King George II of England
Hawaii — King HawaiiLoa
Idaho — Shoshone Indian, "Sun is coming up; it is time to rise"
Illinois — Algonquin Indian, "man, warrior"
Indiana — "Land of Indians"
Iowa — Iowa Indian, "one who puts to sleep"
Kansas — Dakota Indian, "south wind"
Kentucky — Cherokee Indian, "dark and bloody ground"
Louisiana — King Louis XIV of France
Maine — "Mainland"
Maryland — the Blessed Virgin Mary; Queen Henrietta Maria
Massachusetts — Massachusett Indian, "place of great hill"
Michigan — Ojibway Indian, "great lake"
Minnesota — Dakota Indian, "sky-colored waters"
Mississippi — Indian, "father of waters"
Missouri — Indian, "town of large canoes"
Montana — Spanish, "mountainous"
Nebraska — Oto Indian, "flat water"
Nevada — Spanish, "snow clad"
New Hampshire — Hampshire County in England
New Jersey — Isle of Jersey in English Channel
New Mexico — Honoring Mexico
New York — the Duke of York, later King James II of England
North Carolina — King Charles I of England
North Dakota — Dakota Indian, "allies"
Ohio — Iroquois Indian, "something great"
Oklahoma — Choctaw Indian, "people, red"
Oregon — French, "hurricane"
Pennsylvania — [William] Penn; Latin, "woods"
Rhode Island — the Isle of Rhodes in the Aegean Sea
South Carolina — King Charles I of England
South Dakota — Dakota Indian, "allies"
Tennessee — a Cherokee village "Tanasie"
Texas — Tejas Indian, "friendship"
Utah — Ute Indians
Vermont — French, "green mountains"
Virginia — Queen Elizabeth I of England (the "Virgin" Queen)
Washington — George Washington
West Virginia — Queen Elizabeth I of England (the "Virgin" Queen)
Wisconsin — Indian, "gathering of waters" or "wild rice country"
Wyoming — Delaware Indian, "on the great plain"

State Motto

Alabama — We Dare Defend Our Rights
Alaska — North to the Future
Arizona — God Enriches
Arkansas — The People Rule
California — Eureka!
Colorado — Nothing Without Providence
Connecticut — He Who Transplanted Still Sustains
Delaware — Liberty and Independence
Florida — In God We Trust
Georgia — Wisdom, Justice, and Moderation
Hawaii — The Life of the Land is Perpetuated in Righteousness
Idaho — It is Perpetual
Illinois — State Sovereignty, National Union
Indiana — The Crossroads of America
Iowa — Our Liberties We Prize, Our Rights We Will Maintain
Kansas — To the Stars Through Difficulties
Kentucky — United We Stand, Divided We Fall
Louisiana — Union, Justice, and Confidence
Maine — I Direct
Maryland — Manly Deeds, Womanly Words
Massachusetts — By the Sword We Seek Peace, But Peace Only Under Liberty
Michigan — If You Seek a Pleasant Peninsula, Look About You
Minnesota — The Star of the North
Mississippi — By Valor and Arms
Missouri — The Welfare of the People Shall be the Supreme Law
Montana — Gold and Silver
Nebraska — Equality Before the Law
Nevada — All for Our Country
New Hampshire — Live Free or Die
New Jersey — Liberty and Prosperity
New Mexico — It Grows as it Goes
New York — Excelsior
North Carolina — To Be Rather Than To Seem
North Dakota — Liberty and Union, Now and Forever, One and Inseparable
Ohio — With God, All Things are Possible
Oklahoma — Labor Conquers All Things
Oregon — The Union
Pennsylvania — Virtue, Liberty, and Independence
Rhode Island — Hope
South Carolina — While I Breathe, I Hope
South Dakota — Under God the People Rule
Tennessee — Agriculture and Commerce
Texas — Friendship
Utah — Industry
Vermont — Freedom and Unity
Virginia — Thus Always to Tyrants
Washington — By and By
West Virginia — Mountaineers are Always Free
Wisconsin — Forward
Wyoming — Equal Rights

State Industry

Alabama — steel, cotton lint, coal
Alaska — processed fish, dairy, petroleum, mining
Arizona — electrical equipment, cattle, copper, cotton
Arkansas — processed foods, cotton, petroleum
California — machinery, vegetables and fruits, petroleum, electronics, film production
Colorado — machinery, cattle, petroleum, wheat
Connecticut — machinery, dairy, soybeans, stone
Delaware — chemicals, broiler chickens, sand and gravel
Florida — processed foods, oranges, phosphate, tourism
Georgia — textile mill products, broiler chickens, clays
Hawaii — processed foods, sugarcane, sand and gravel, tourism
Idaho — processed foods, potatoes, cattle, silver
Illinois — steel, corn, coal
Indiana — electrical equipment, corn, coal, hogs
Iowa — nonelectric machinery, hogs, stone, corn
Kansas — transportation equipment, wheat, petroleum, cattle
Kentucky — whiskey, tobacco, coal, cattle
Louisiana — chemicals, rice, petroleum
Maine — paper products, potatoes, cement, seafood
Maryland — food products, poultry, seafood, coal
Massachusetts — electrical equipment, dairy, sand and gravel, seafood
Michigan — motor vehicles, dairy, iron ore, fruit
Minnesota — chemicals, corn, iron ore
Mississippi — clothing, cotton, petroleum
Missouri — transportation equipment, soybeans, lead
Montana — copper products, cattle, copper, wheat
Nebraska — food products, cattle, petroleum
Nevada — food products, cattle, barite, tourism
New Hampshire — nonelectrical equipment, dairy, sand and gravel
New Jersey — chemicals, vegetables and fruits , stone
New Mexico — petroleum, cattle, natural gas
New York — printing and publishing, dairy, stone
North Carolina — textiles, tobacco, stone
North Dakota — machinery, wheat, petroleum
Ohio — transportation equipment, corn, coal
Oklahoma — nonelectric machinery, cattle, petroleum
Oregon — wood products, cattle, sand and gravel
Pennsylvania — metal foundry industries, dairy, coal
Rhode Island — metal foundries, dairy
South Carolina — textile mill products, tobacco, cement
South Dakota — food products, cattle, gold
Tennessee — chemicals, tobacco, stone
Texas — chemicals, cattle, petroleum
Utah — food products, barley, asphalt, mining
Vermont — machines and tools, dairy, granite
Virginia — chemicals, cattle, coal, dairy
Washington — aircraft and aerospace systems, wheat, coal, timber
West Virginia — chemicals, dairy, coal
Wisconsin — engines, dairy, sand and gravel
Wyoming — petroleum products, cattle, petroleum

ALABAMA
For the Alibamu Indians

State Nickname
The Yellowhammer State

State Landmark
Tuskegee Institute

Capital
Montgomery

Famous Native
Helen Keller

State Tree
Southern Pine

Historical Fact: Montgomery was 1st Confederate capital

Catholic Fact: Ave Maria Grotto replicas

State Bird

Yellowhammer

State Flower

Camellia

Industries: Manufactured goods: steel; Agricultural goods: cotton lint; Mineral: coal

Area: 29th in size, 51,705 square miles

Date of Admission: December 14, 1819 (22nd)

State Motto: We Dare Defend Our Rights

State Nickname **State Landmark** **Capital**

Famous Native **State Tree**

Historical Fact:

Catholic Fact:

State Bird

State Flower

Extra Credit

Industries:

Area:

Date of Admission:

State Motto:

Alabama

Alaska

Arizona

Arkansas

California

Colorado

Connecticut

Delaware

Florida

Georgia

Hawaii

Idaho

Illinois

Indiana

Iowa

Kansas

Kentucky

Louisiana

Maine

Maryland

Massachusetts   Michigan   Minnesota   Mississippi

Missouri   Montana   Nebraska   Nevada

New Hampshire   New Jersey   New Mexico   New York

North Carolina   North Dakota   Ohio   Oklahoma

Oregon   Pennsylvania   Rhode Island   South Carolina

South Dakota

Tennessee

Texas

Utah

Vermont

Virginia

Washington

West Virginia

Wisconsin

Wyoming

Alabama

Alaska

Arizona

Arkansas

California

Colorado

Connecticut

Delaware

Florida

Georgia

Hawaii

Idaho

Illinois

Indiana

Iowa

Kansas

Kentucky

Louisiana

Maine

Maryland

Massachusetts

Michigan

Minnesota

Mississippi

Missouri

Montana

Nebraska

Nevada

New Hampshire

New Jersey

New Mexico

New York

North Carolina

North Dakota

Ohio

Oklahoma

Oregon

Pennsylvania

Rhode Island

South Carolina

South Dakota

Tennessee

Texas

Utah

Vermont

Virginia

Washington

West Virginia

Wisconsin

Wyoming

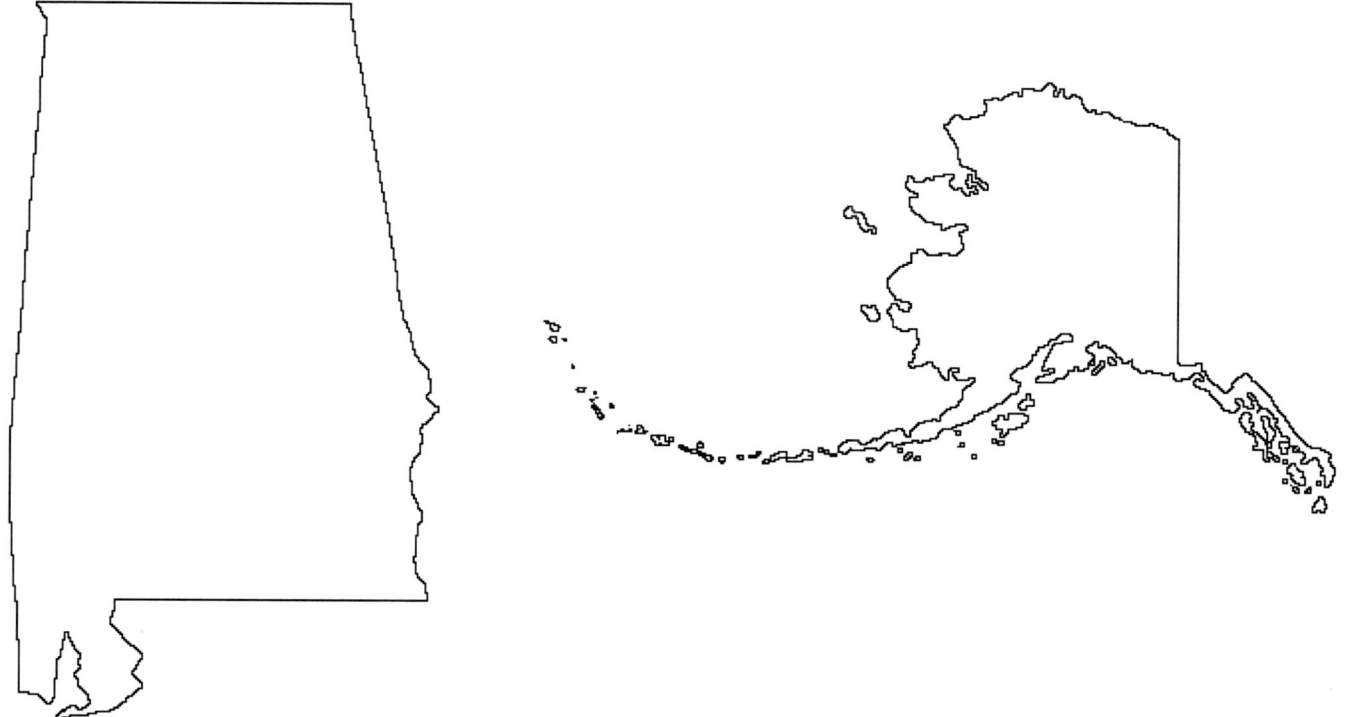

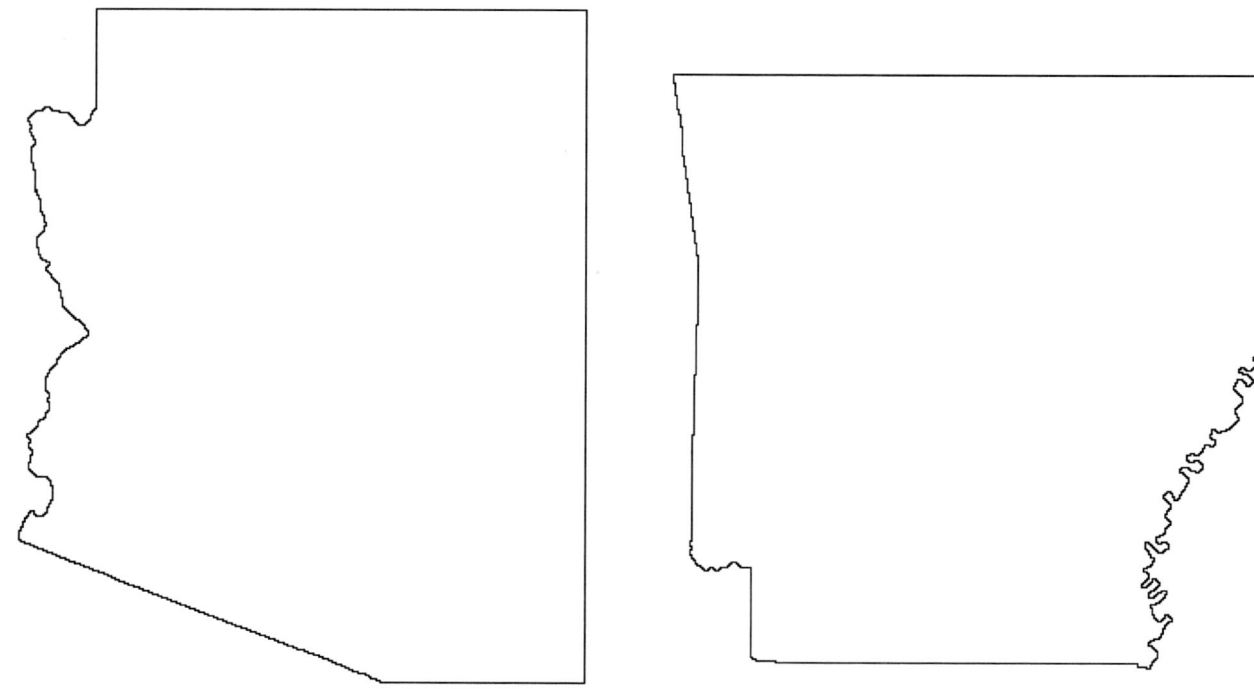

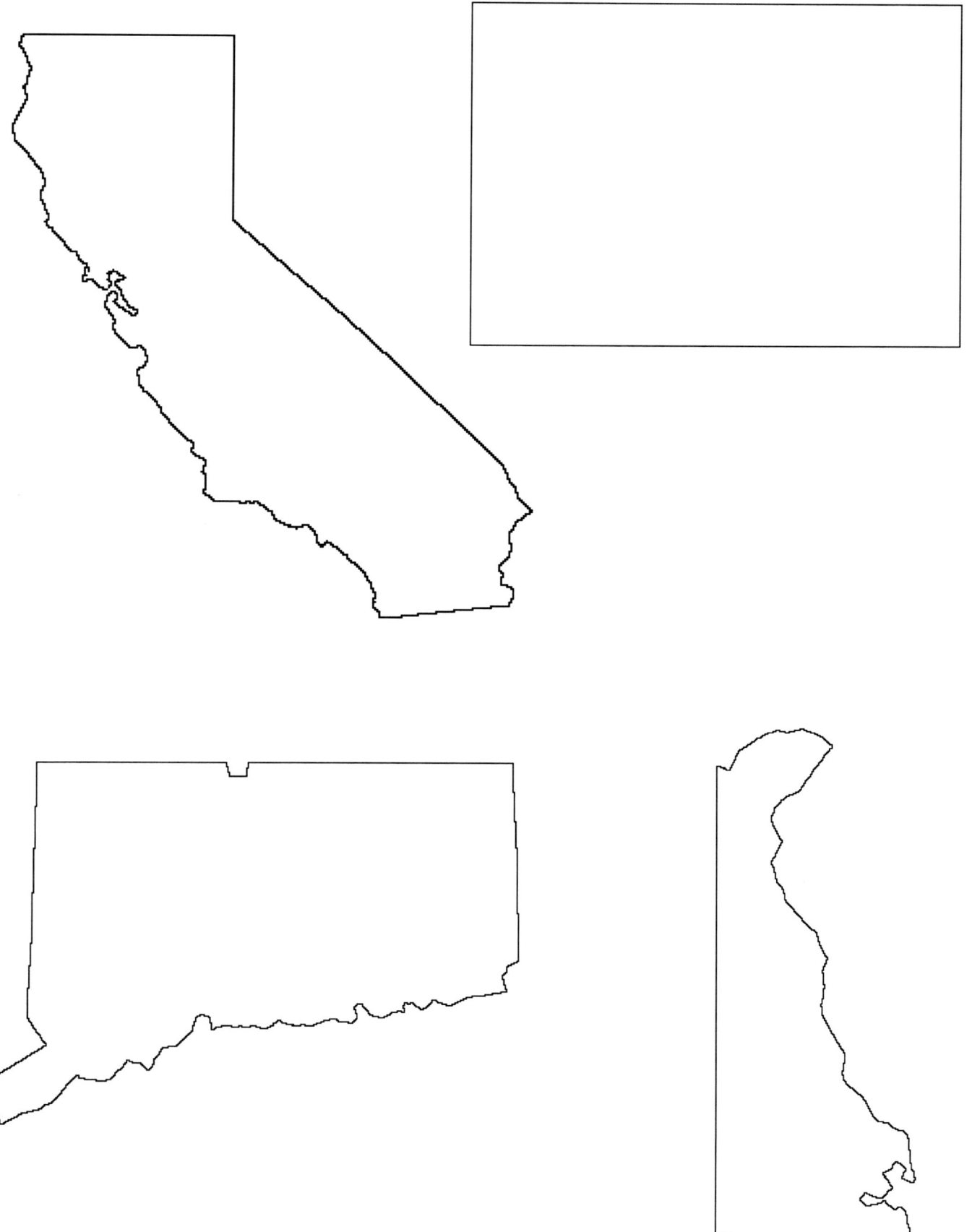

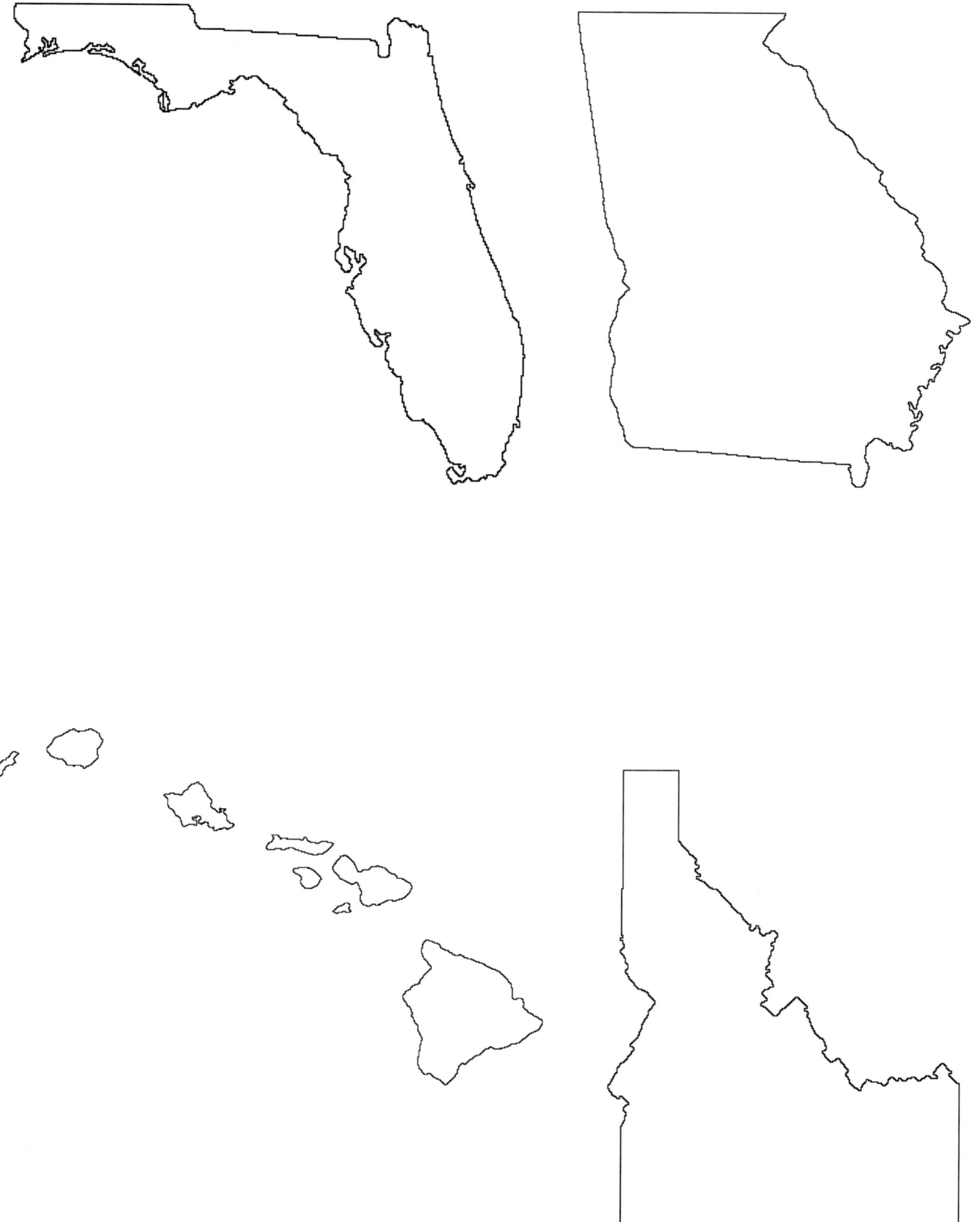

77

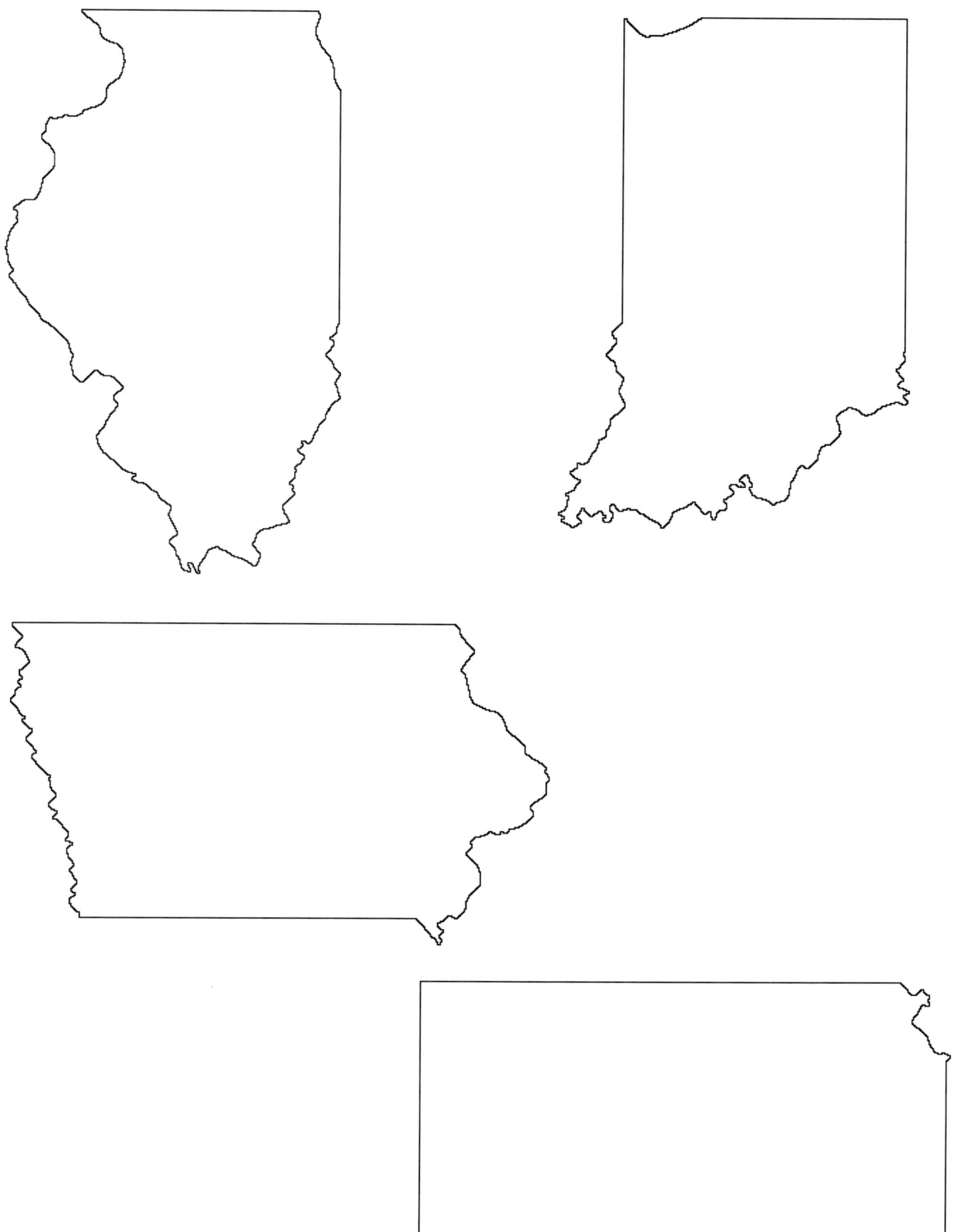

79

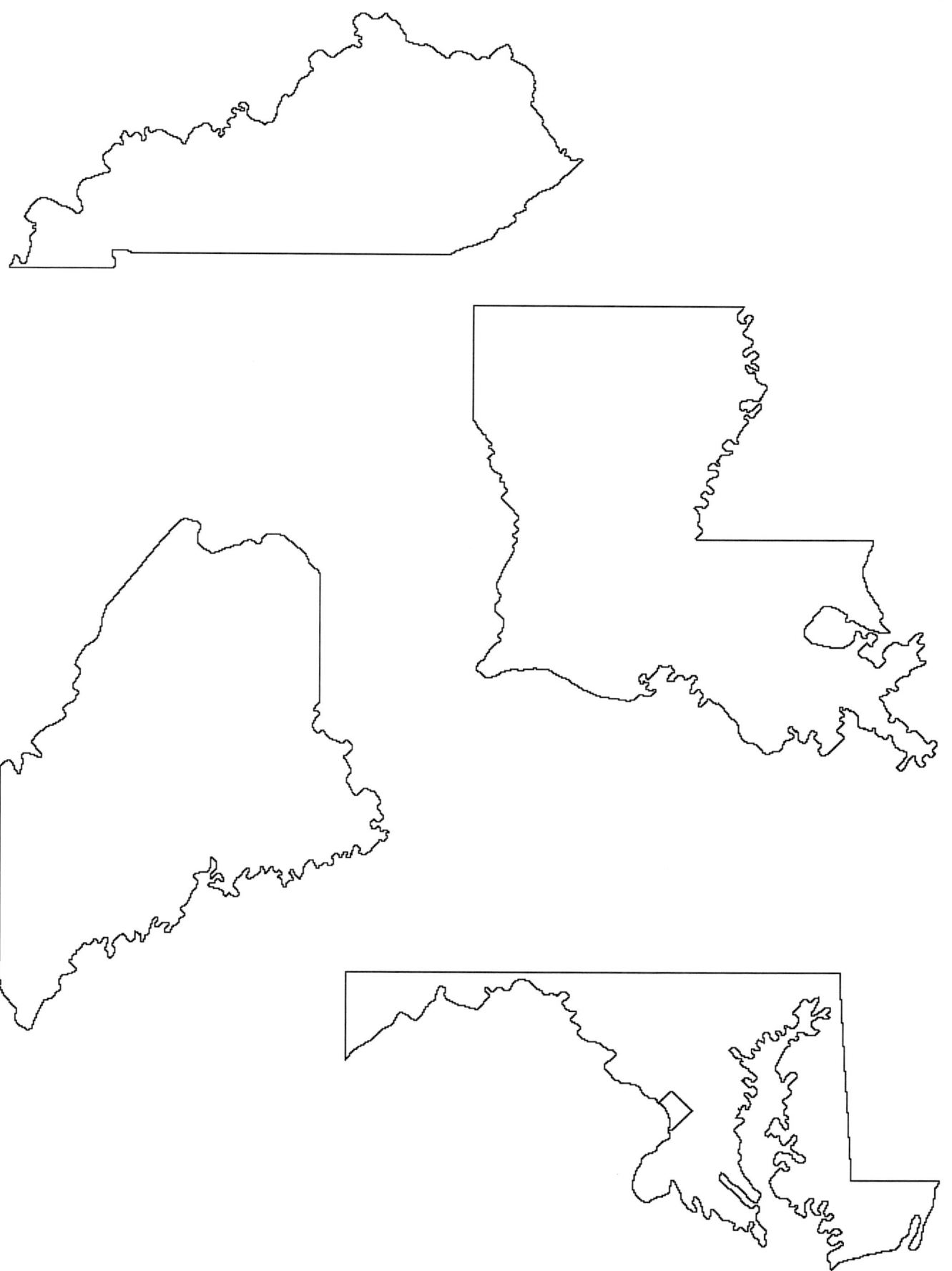

81

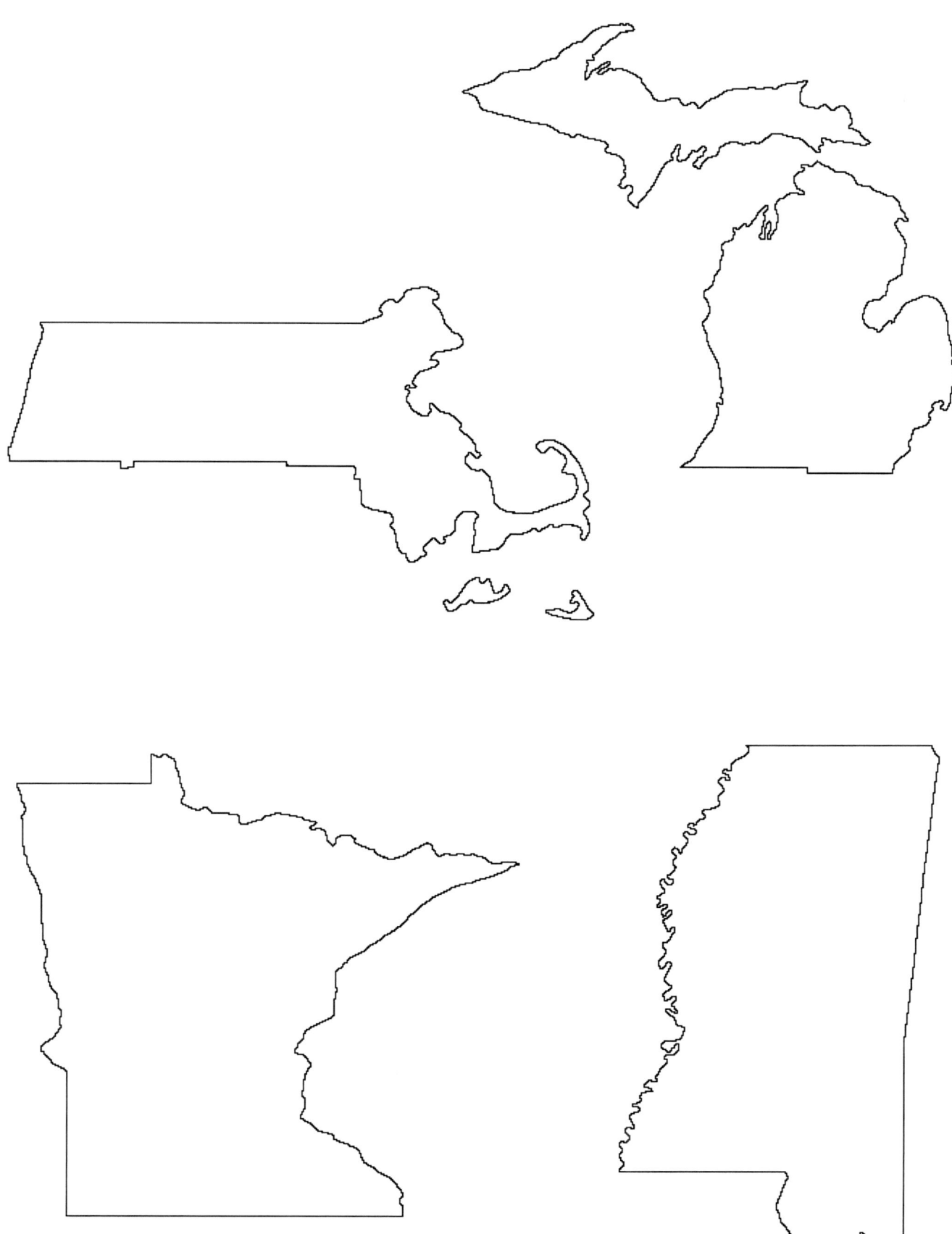

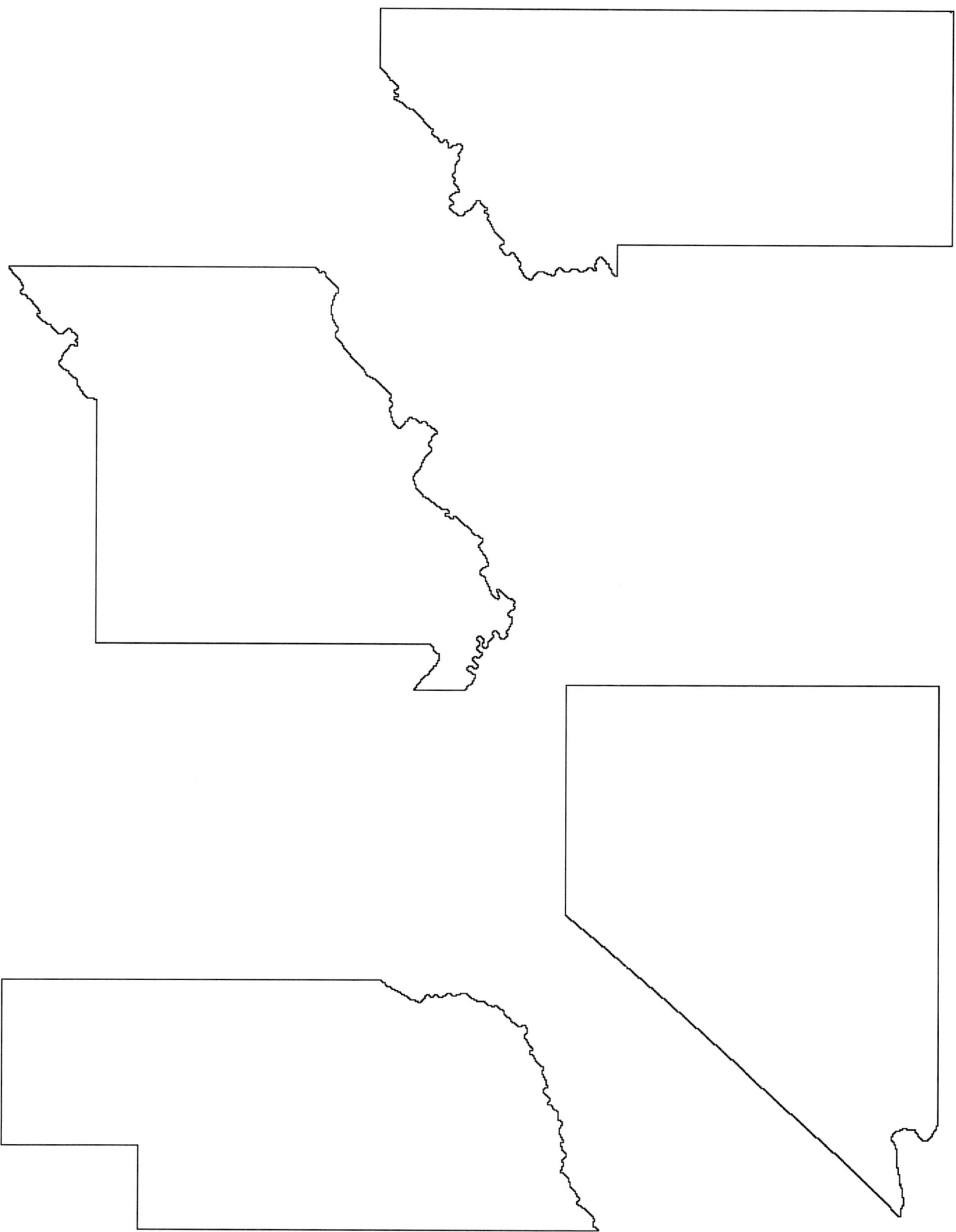

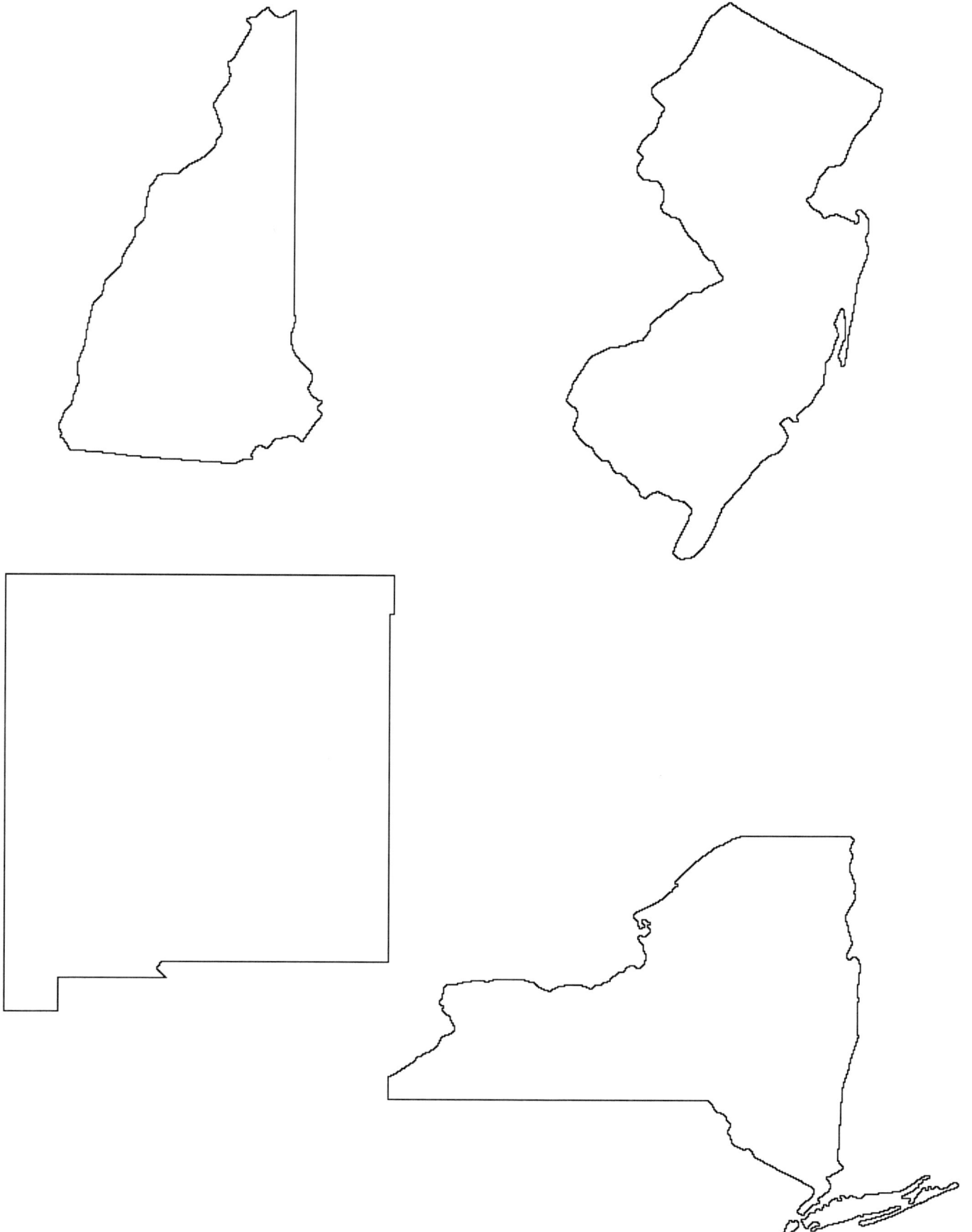

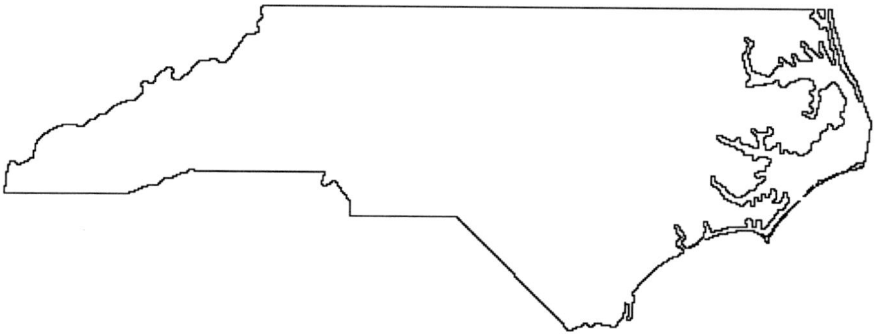

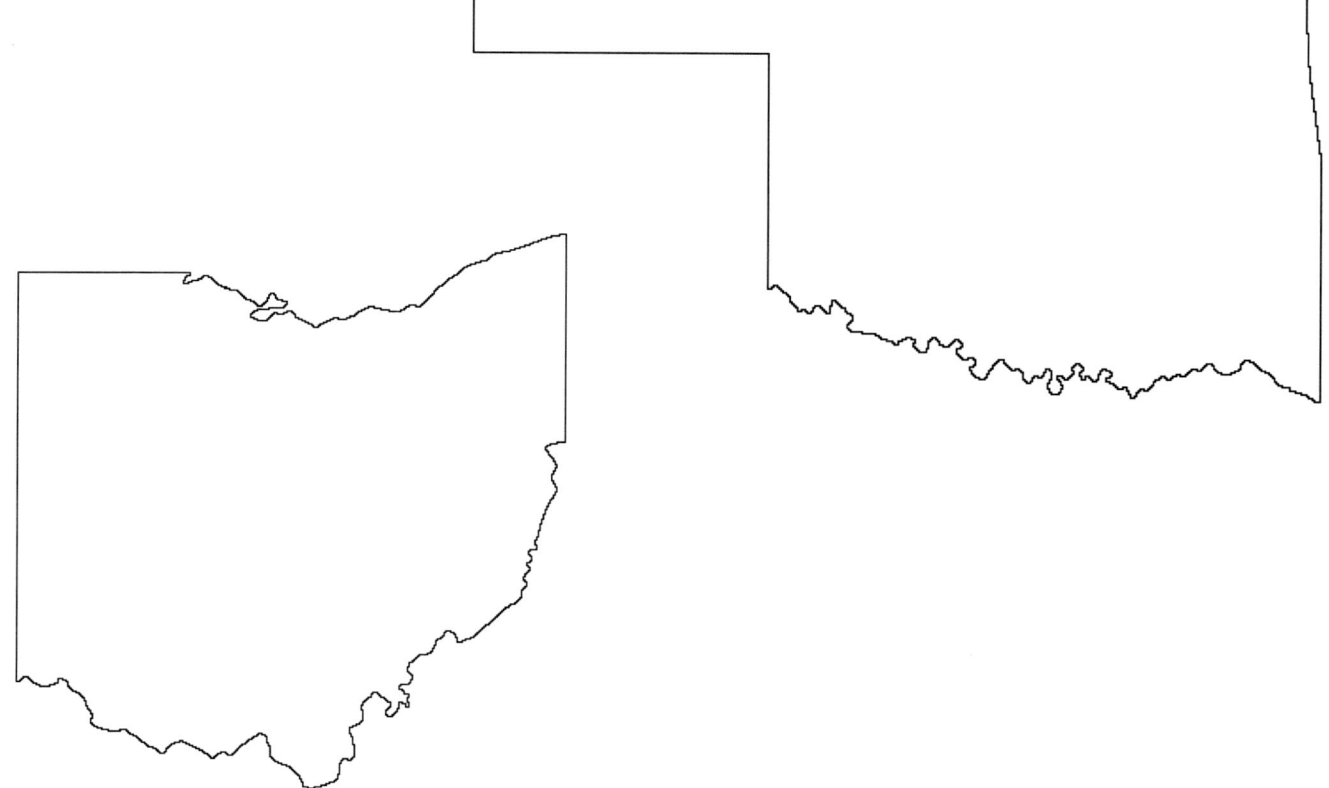

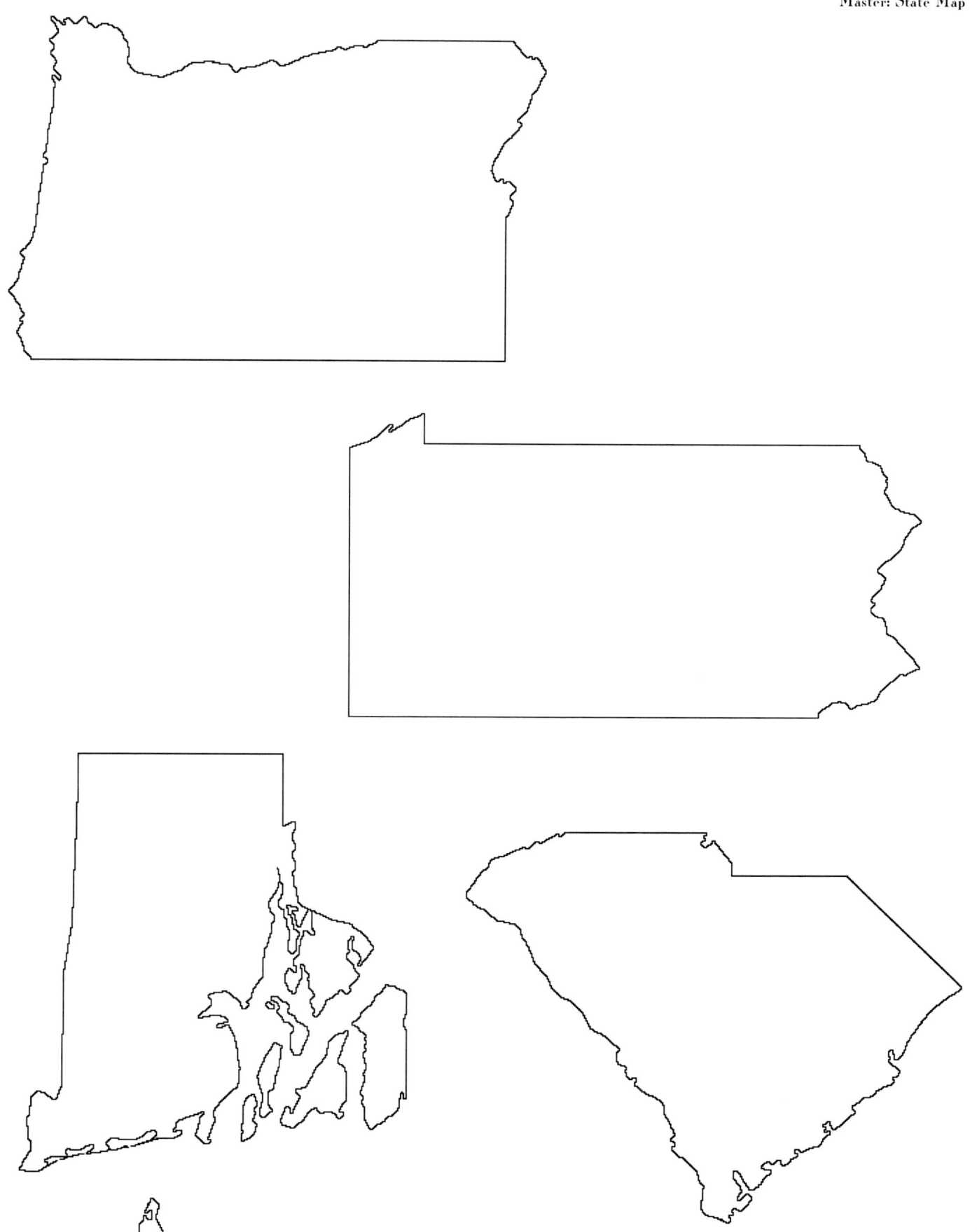

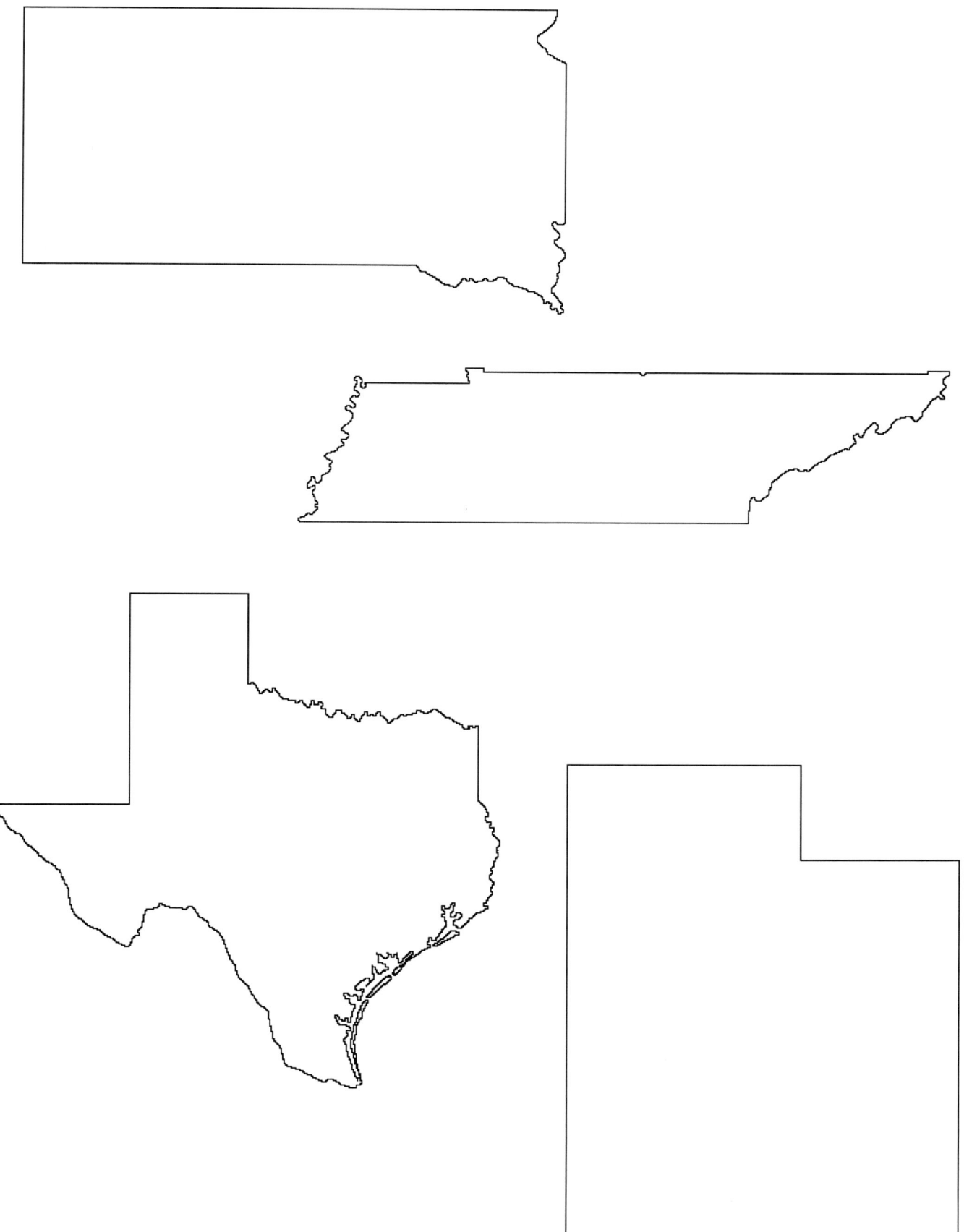

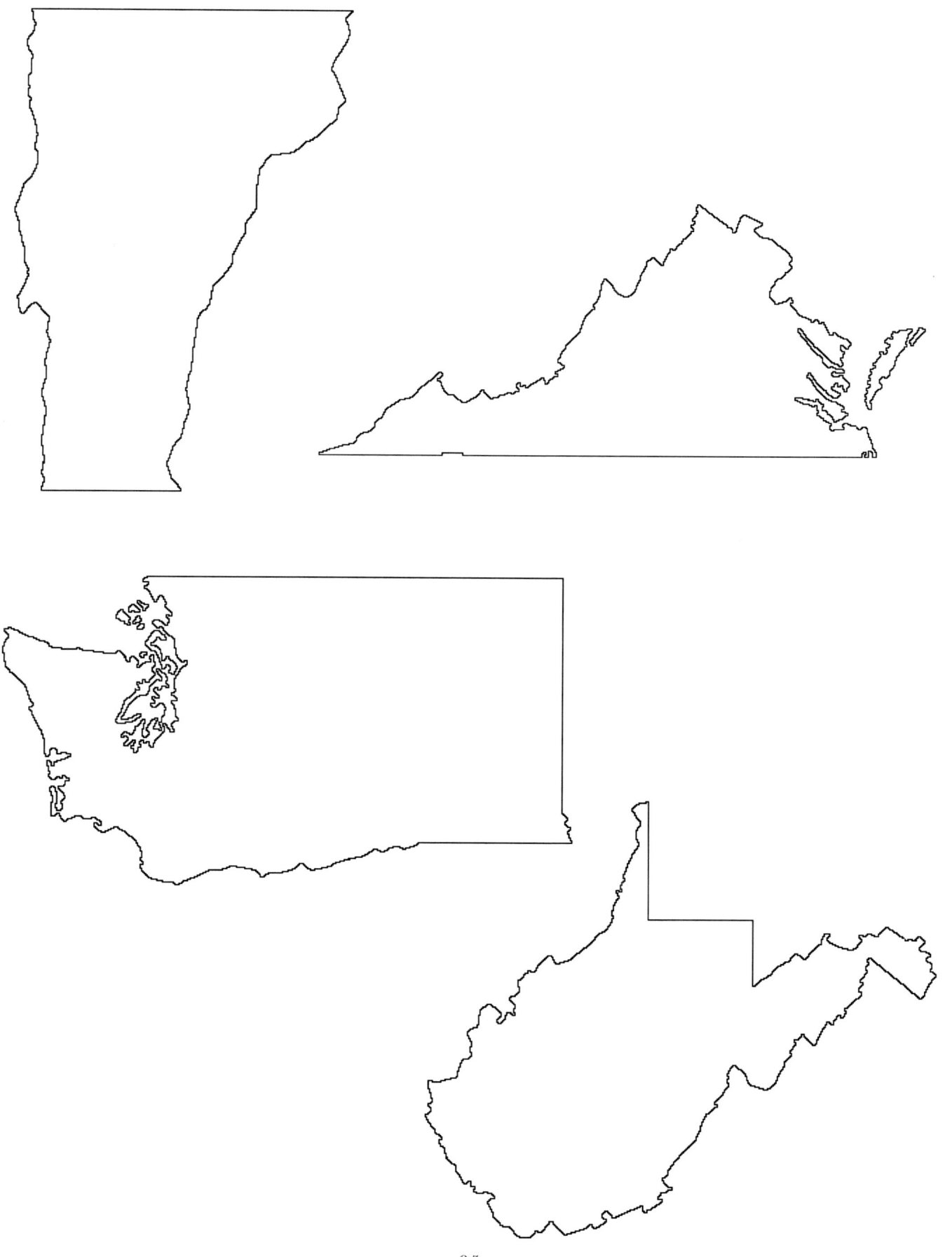

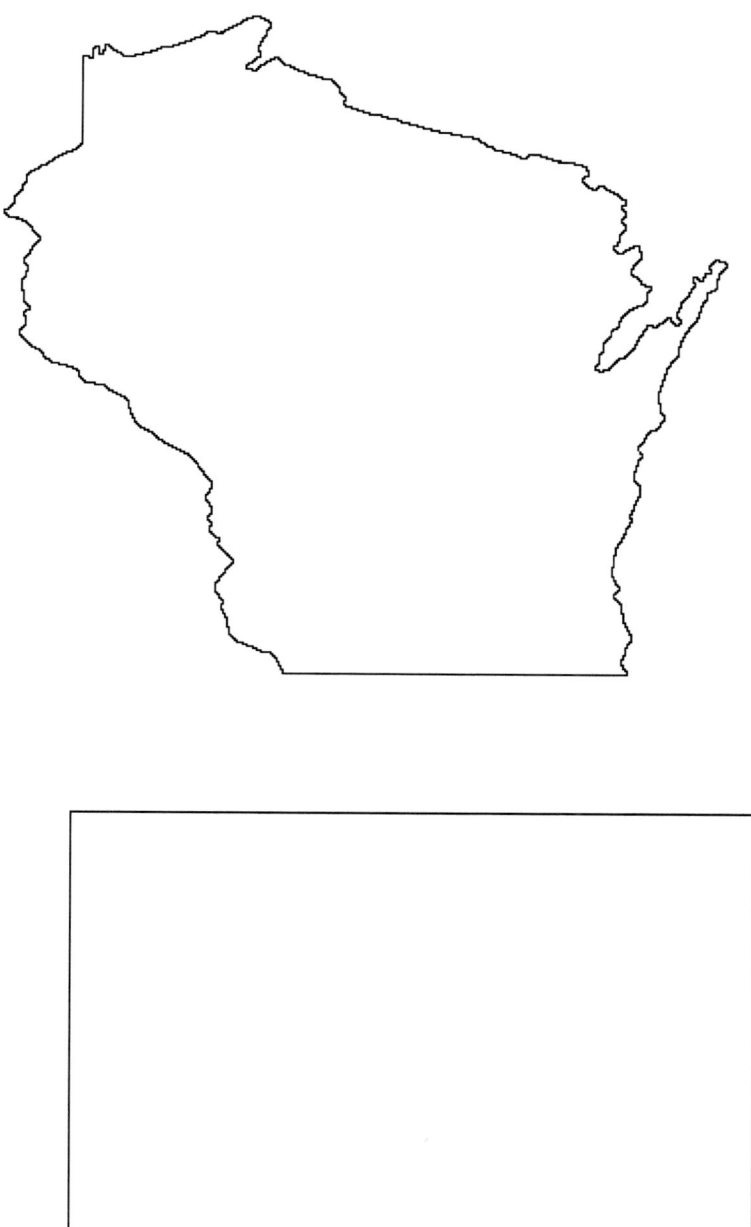

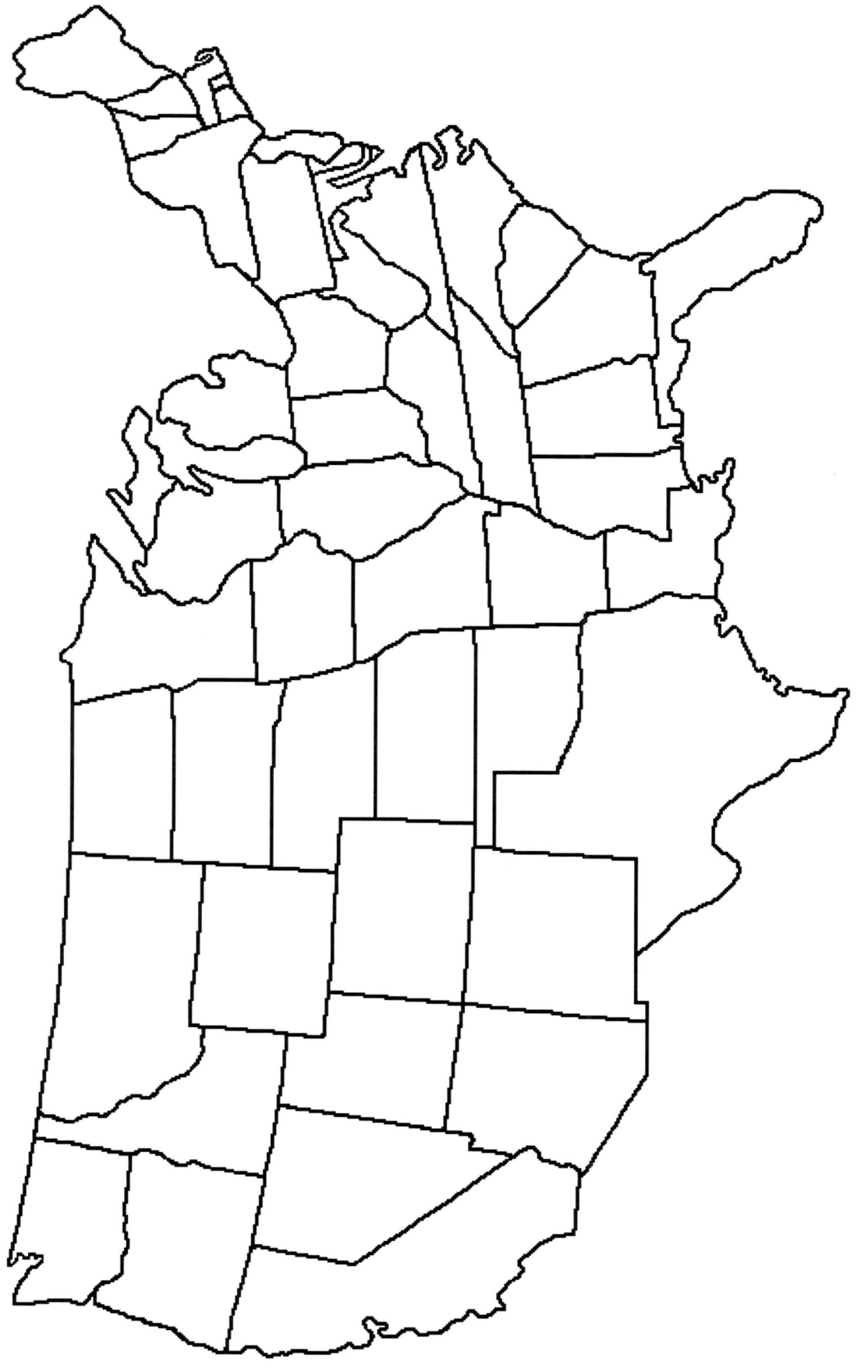

Mary Immaculate,
Patroness of the United States, pray for us!

Dianne Gotay

"... So, then, it was that the Immaculate Conception became officially the great Patroness of the vast union of States that had sprung up in the New World."

For every American Catholic the year 1846 should be one of the most memorable dates [on the] historic calendar. It is the year in which the Sixth Provincial Council of Baltimore solemnly requested the Holy See to approve of its selction of "Mary Conceived without Sin" as Patroness of the United States. [Rome granted the permission in 1847.]

Be it carefully noted that the peculiar phrasing itself of Mary's title by the assembled American prelates must obviously lead to the conclusion that it was taken by them, literally and directly, from the petition inscribed on the Miraculous Medal: "O Mary, conceived without sin, pray for us who have recourse to you." So, then, it was that the Immaculate Conception, "Mary Conceived without Sin," Mary Immaculate, became officially the great Patroness of the vast union of States that had sprung up in the New World. And that world itself...had been discovered by one of the most devoted apostles of Mary's privilege, Columbus.

"Conception," "Port Conception," "Holy Mary of the Immaculate Conception," were names he gave to islands or ports that he discovered. Worthy, too, of special notice is the fact that on his famous second voyage Columbus formally placed himself directly under the protection of the Immaculate Conception....

We have thus come in our historical account to the memorable year 1846. Just another eight years elapsed, and there followed at Rome, on December 8, 1854, the solemn declaration, by Pope Pius IX, of the Immaculate Conception of Mary...:

We declare, pronounce and define that the doctrine which holds that the Blessed Virgin Mary, at the first instant of her conception, by a singular privilege and grace of the Omnipotent God, in virtue of the merits of Jesus Christ, the Saviour of mankind, was preserved immaculate from all stain of original sin, has been revealed by God, and therefore should firmly and constantly be believed by all the Faithful.

Excerpts from an article by Joseph Husslein, SJ, 1930.

A Toast to the Flag

Here's to the RED of it -
Apostles' spread of it,
Millions are dead for it,
Virgins have shed for it,
    Proves what Christ said.
Martyrs have bled for it,
Lost limb and head for it,
Faced fire and lead for it,
    Bathing it red!
Here's to the WHITE of it -
Oh! just the sight of it,
The brilliant light of it,
Makes nations fight for it,
    Through day and night.
Humanity's share of it,
Christ Our Lord's care of it,
Purity's prayer for it
    Preserves it white!
Here's to the BLUE of it -
Our Lady's view of it
Motherly hue of it,
Queenly care, too, of it
    Constant and true;
Brothers embrace for it
No select race for it
Only one place for it
    Under her blue!

Adapted from "A Toast to the Flag."

Catholic-Named Cities of the United States

These actual towns reveal the influence
of the Catholic Church in the development of our country.
Can you find these and others on your map?

Holy Trinity, Alabama

St. Marys, Alaska

St. Michael, Arizona

St. Francis, Arkansas

Los Angeles, California

St. Louis, Colorado

Bethany, Connecticut

Mission, Delaware

St. Augustine, Florida

St. George, Georgia

Molokai, Hawaii (Fr. Damien's leper colony)

Priest, Idaho

Assumption, Illinois

St. Mary-of-the-Woods, Indiana

Holy Cross, Iowa

St. Paul, Kansas

Trappist, Kentucky

Jesuit Bend, Louisiana

Pulpit Harbor, Maine

St. Mary's City, Maryland

MASSachusetts

St. Charles, Michigan

Holy Family, Minnesota

Friar Point, Mississippi

St. Peter, Missouri

St. Ignatius, Montana

Abbott, Nebraska

Paradise Valley, Nevada

Temple, New Hampshire

Deacons, New Jersey

Santa Fe, New Mexico

Rome, New York

Pope, North Carolina

St. Thomas, North Dakota

Blessings, Ohio

Sacred Heart, Oklahoma

St. Helens, Oregon

Mt. Carmel, Pennsylvania

Providence, Rhode Island

Angelus, South Carolina

De Smet, South Dakota

St. Joseph, Tennessee

Corpus Christi, Texas

St. Clara, Utah

St. Albert, Vermont

St. Stephen's Church, Virginia

St. John, Washington

Three Churches, West Virginia

Mt. Calvary, Wisconsin

St. Stephen, Wyoming

Our sincere thanks to Miss Therese Lawrence for sharing the fruits of her extensive research.

Bibliography

The World Book Encyclopedia. Chicago: World Book-Childcraft.

Encyclopedia Americana. NY: Americana Corp.

The Catholic Encyclopedia. NY: Gilmary Society, 1910.

Kane, Joseph, Steven Anzovin and Janet Podell, eds. *Facts About the States.* 2nd ed., NY: H.W. Wilson, 1993.

Moran, J. Anthony. *Pilgrims' Guide to America.* Huntington, IN: Our Sunday Visitor, 1992.

Sources for Further Study

Vision Book Series (Father Kino, Katharine Drexel, Governor Al Smith, Kit Carson of the Old West, Rose Hawthorne, Mother Cabrini, Frances Warde, Father Damien and the Bells, Mother Seton and the Sisters of Charity, A Cross in the West, John Carroll, St. Isaac and the Indians, Father Marquette and the Great Rivers). Farrar, Straus, & Company, 1960s. Ignatius Press is reprinting some titles.

Bunson, Margaret, and Stephen Bunson. *Faith in the Wilderness.* Huntington, IL: Our Sunday Visitor, 2000.

Carroll, Anne W. *Christ and the Americas.* Rockford, IL: TAN Books, 1997.

Furlong, Philip J. *Our Pioneers and Patriots.* Rockford, IL: TAN Books, 1997.

Leek, James R. *Evangelization of the New World.* Olathe, KS: St. Paul's Publishing, 1987.

Myers, Rawley. *American Women of Faith.* Huntington, IN: Our Sunday Visitor, 1989.

Nevins, Albert J. *Builders of Catholic America.* Huntington, IN: Our Sunday Visitor, 1985.

---. *Our American Catholic Heritage.* Huntington, IN: Our Sunday Visitor, 1972.

Internet Sites for Further Study

reference page 15   Mary Garden: www.mgardens.org

reference page 37   Grotto of the Redemption: www.westbendgrotto.com

reference page 43   Ave Maria Grotto: www.avemariagrotto.com

reference page 45   Catholics in American History: www.chcweb.com/catalog/freecurricula.html

Basilica of the National Shrine of the Immaculate Conception (make a virtual tour of the "Hall of American Saints"): www.nationalshrine.com

reference pgs. 61-71 50 States.Com (resource for coloring the State Bird and Flower images): www.50states.com (children should use with supervision)

reference page 99   Color Landform Atlas of the United States: http://fermi.jhuapl.edu/states/states.html

reference page 99   Outline Maps: http://www.eduplace.com/ss/ssmaps/index.html

CPSIA information can be obtained at www.ICGtesting.com
Printed in the USA
BVOW062128181011

273985BV00001B/35/P